MODERN ECONOMIC ISSUES

OTTO ECKSTEIN, *Harvard University, General Editor*

In this series the great public issues in economics are posed and put in perspective by original commentary and reprints of the most interesting and significant recent statements by experts in economics and government.

ALSO IN THE MODERN ECONOMIC ISSUES SERIES

American Fiscal Policy: Experiment for Prosperity,
edited by Lester C. Thurow

City and Suburb: The Economics of Metropolitan Growth,
edited by Benjamin Chinitz

The Common Market: Progress and Controversy,
edited by Lawrence B. Krause

Controlling Pollution: The Economics of a Cleaner America,
edited by Marshall I. Goldman

Defense and Disarmament: The Economics of Transition,
edited by Roger E. Bolton

Economic Growth: An American Problem,
edited by Peter M. Gutmann

The Economics of Poverty: An American Paradox,
edited by Burton A. Weisbrod

Men Without Work: The Economics of Unemployment,
edited by Stanley Lebergott

RICHARD E. LOW, the editor of this volume in the Modern Economic Issues series, is both an economist and a lawyer. An Associate Professor of Economics at the Rutgers University Graduate School and a member of the New York Bar, he was graduated (A.B. *summa cum laude*) from Princeton University and holds an LL.B. from New York University and an M.A. and Ph.D. from Harvard University. Among his publications are *The Development of Executive Talents* (co-author, 1958), *The Ownership of Unforeseen Rights* (1964), the forthcoming *American Economic Organization* and *Competition in Theory and Practice,* and a number of antitrust articles in the learned journals. He was formerly an economist with the United States Chamber of Commerce and the American Management Association and on the faculties of Pennsylvania State University and the City University of New York.

THE ECONOMICS OF ANTITRUST

Competition and Monopoly

THE ECONOMICS
OF ANTITRUST

COMPETITION AND MONOPOLY

Edited by Richard E. Low

 PRENTICE-HALL, Inc., Englewood Cliffs, N.J.

CONTENTS

THE ECONOMICS OF ANTITRUST

Competition and Monopoly

INTRODUCTION

Antitrust is in many ways a bridge between different disciplines and different national goals. Two areas of academic specialization, economics and law, are both deeply involved in the analysis and solution of antitrust problems. Among our national goals, the maintenance of competition is joined with the preservation of small business, the promotion of high employment and economic growth, and the continuation of the postwar battle against inflation.

But a bridge does more than connect separate points. It permits the wayfarer to avoid the river or the chasm beneath—but only as long as he does in fact reach the opposite side. Nothing is more useless than a ten-foot bridge for a twenty-foot divide. Indeed, it may be worse than useless, since it creates a false sense of security by leading the traveler on for ten feet of roadway before disappearing under his feet. Such false security may be the result of unwise antitrust policies. And indeed, considering the widespread division of informed opinion concerning almost all antitrust issues, a false sense of economic security may well be the practical result of some of our policies.

Such differences of opinion are not, of course, unique in antitrust. What is perhaps unique is the length of time during which no conclusion or informed consensus has been reached. This is probably a result of the failure of antitrust issues to arouse the same degree of national debate that has attended American policies on economic growth, inflation and employment. Antitrust issues appear too complex for personal attention to many people, and there is a tendency to leave the subject to the experts. Without widespread debate, it is hard to obtain resolution.

The failure of a national consensus to appear is also probably a result, in part, of the fact that antitrust issues, alone among national economic ones, can be reduced to judicial cases subject to court decision. This might seem to make such issues signally adapted to decision. But the Supreme Court has shown no more consistency in this area than it has in many others. The present Supreme Court is often divided five to four on most major antitrust issues,[1] a division ill adapted to general confidence in the permanence of its antitrust opinions.

Thus antitrust—despite its seniority among national economic goals and eighty years of developing standards—remains an area of controversial issues and of divergent goals. These issues and goals will form the subject matter of this essay.

ANTITRUST, MARKET STRUCTURES AND NATIONAL ECONOMIC GOALS

We as a people have three national economic goals: price stability and economic growth, both encouraged under the Federal Reserve Act of 1913, and the high level of employment added to these two by the Employment Act of 1946. Antitrust is intricately connected with price stability and economic growth. It influences as well, although to a lesser degree, the level of employment. These connections operate mainly through antitrust's influence on our economic market structures.

Antitrust and Market Structure

Economic theory possesses four models of the economy which, through their usefulness as abstract standards rather than through the frequency of their appearance in the economy, are helpful in furthering our economic understanding. The traditional model is pure competition, an early product of classical economic thought—frequently, but incorrectly, taken to be an approximation of what the economy actually is or should be.

Pure Competition

Pure competition is, in a sense, the *beau ideal* of some antitrust advocates. A purely competitive market is one with so many sellers, and those of so small a size, that no single seller can influence prices or significantly influence the total supply. The product each seller produces must be identical—otherwise customers would be able to distinguish among them and sellers would have some control over the price. No firm advertises, since each sells as much as he wants at the market price. Entry into the market by new competitors is easy and inexpensive. Agriculture, in the absence of government price and production controls, is the nearest approximation of pure competition we find in reality.

Pure competition attains its *beau ideal* status because the pressure of competition on each producer is such that he must constantly seek new ways to cut his costs and must usually make do with the minimum profit necessary for him to remain in business. Thus, it scores high in regard to short term efficiency based on cost-reduction and receives an extra commendation from those hostile to high profits.

But its rarity in the real economy is here to stay, for the large number of firms required depends on sharply rising unit costs after minimum cost is reached, keeping firms small. Outside of agriculture and retailing, such rising unit costs are uncommon. Small, purely competitive firms do not have the power to violate the antitrust laws, but this advantage must remain unrealized.

Monopolistic Competition

Monopolistic competition shares with pure competition the characteristics of small and multiple firms, easy entry into the industry and sharply rising unit costs. But, unlike pure competition, the products sold by these firms vary somewhat from each other, and thus the seller has some control over the price he charges. It thus pays each firm to advertise. Monopolistic competition is found primarily in retailing, where geographical differences, and their related consumer convenience, prevent products from being identical; that is, a consumer has a decided preference between toothpaste sold a block away and the identical brand sold four blocks away—a preference a better located store can capitalize on through higher prices.

Monopolistic competition has a bad name among economists;[2] the higher prices reflect higher costs, since each firm, by raising prices, operates at a lower output than the output providing minimum costs. Further, retailers have managed to obtain special treatment for themselves in antitrust under the Robinson-Patman Act, discussed below, and its restrictions on price discrimination favoring larger firms. But it may be that this hostile view is partly unfair; the product differentiation created under monopolistic competition probably adds to consumer satisfaction in ways beyond the reach of economics to measure.

Unlike pure competition, monopolistically competitive industries play a large share in antitrust. The large number of sellers prevents much in the way of conspiracy violations under Section 1 of the Sherman Act, as discussed below, but retailing has many price discrimination, exclusive dealing and merger cases. The tendency of the courts to favor in these cases the small competitors of monopolist competition over their larger rivals, or possible successors,[3] is one area where antitrust law does not clearly conform to economic theory.

Oligopoly

Oligopolistic industries, characterized by a few large sellers who set their own prices, by difficult entry, declining unit costs, advertising, and either identical or differentiated products, are typical of the American economy. Automobiles, steel, aluminum, computers and many other essential American products are manufactured under such conditions.

Further, oligopoly plays a leading role in antitrust, since the interdependence of the few large manufacturers on each other makes them possible violators of all antitrust provisions, from conspiracy to mergers.

It is in this area of theory that differences of view among economists are most pronounced and most important to antitrust. Are oligopolistic industries beneficial or should they provide antitrust with its main enemy? The more traditional view ascribes to oligopoly high prices, lower output, substantial profits and hostility to any form of progress that might threaten the dominance of the leading firms. But this view has been widely attacked. One view, intellectually founded by the late American-Austrian Harvard economist,

Joseph A. Schumpeter, believes that high profits are necessary to finance research and development, and that power over its own price by each firm is necessary to encourage innovations and to allow the innovator to profit from them.[4] Another group, more practical in approach, believes that empirical evidence shows oligopolies to be characterized by large output prices near the competitive level and substantial progress.[5] This latter view has led to the radical work of the Princeton economist, William Baumol, who believes that oligopolies aim not at profit maximization but at sales maximization, thus in part combining the advantages of pure competition with those of size.[6] These economists share an emphasis on long-term growth over short-term efficiency.

Monopoly

Monopoly possesses every characteristic but one for playing the role of the primary villain in antitrust. With a market characterized by only one seller setting his own price, difficult or impossible entry into the industry, decreasing costs, and a product either undifferentiated or differentiated (possibly into several products each constituting a separate monopoly), the utter lack of direct competition would seem to make this market structure antitrust's main enemy.

The one characteristic saving it from this fate, in actuality, is lack of government regulation; in the United States, monopolies and their prices are—except sometimes, when only local—under government supervision. This does not prevent antitrust problems, since exclusive dealing, price discrimination and other cases do arise, but it does limit the importance of monopolies in antitrust law.

MARKET STRUCTURE CHANGES AND ANTITRUST ACHIEVEMENTS

Antitrust plays a prominent role, in relation to our main, national, economic objectives, as a "policeman" of existing market structures. To the degree that it prevents independent oligopolists from operating through collusive agreements on prices and output, and prevents the rare unregulated monopoly from fully exploiting its customers, suppliers and distributors, it contributes greatly to price stability, economic growth and, to a lesser degree, employment, as discussed below.

But antitrust also plays a more radical role in relation to these national economic objectives. To the degree that it changes our market structures, its effects may be revolutionary indeed.

Substitution of Oligopoly for Monopoly

As has been argued by University of Chicago economist, George Stigler, our antitrust policies have replaced monopoly, and incipient monopoly, with oligopoly as our dominant industrial market structure.[7]

This argument can be supported by a host of historical evidence. Oil, tobacco, steel and many other leading products were produced by monopolies, or near monopolies, in the early part of this century, until these monopolies were dissolved by the application of antitrust suits[8] or by the passage of time. According to Professor Stigler, and he seems to have logic on his side, time proved as effective as it did only because of the ever-present threat of antitrust.[9] The power of monopolies and of cartels in modern economies without our antitrust policies substantiates this belief.[10]

This effect of antitrust is revolutionary in two separate ways. First, even the most hostile critic of oligopoly will usually admit that its record in pricing, output and economic progress is far better than that of monopoly. Thus the beneficial effects on economic growth, price stability and employment have been great even by these sceptical standards; how much greater must they be in the view of those who believe oligopoly to be economically progressive and to approach purely competitive pricing and output.

Second, the political effects of this revolution cannot be understated. The regulation of monopoly in the United States is accepted policy; if our industrial sector were monopolized, its regulation would probably follow. How powerful would the federal government now be if our major industries were directed, or even regulated, by Washington. Whether our democratic form of society could even survive such a concentration of power seems to the author doubtful. Those who are sceptical of government efficiency might also believe that such regulation would end, or substantially reduce, our economic progress and growth.

Less Concentrated Oligopolies

⌐A second market structure change probably affected by antitrust is the replacement of some highly concentrated oligopolies by less concentrated ones. Such, according to the Supreme Court, is a desirable objective of antitrust.[11] One example would be the motion picture industry.[12]⌐

Such a change would have two main results. First, it would lessen the chances of collusive antitrust violations, since collusion is much more difficult among many conspirators than among only several. Second, and more significantly, it would greatly increase the competitive pressure upon our oligopolists, assuming, as seems logical, that ten competitors cause more loss of sleep than one or two. Thus the pressure upon big business to innovate, to hold prices down and otherwise to perform better economically would be increased.

Monopolistic Competition for Oligopoly

A third possible market structure change is much more questionable in its desirability. Has antitrust caused oligopoly, or potential oligopoly, to be superseded by new or continuing monopolistic competition? If so, the ill repute of this latter market structure among economists would seem to hold this result up to question.

Two areas of antitrust law share the alleged villain's role here. First, the Robinson-Patman Act, passed in 1936 under pressure from threatened and frightened small retailers, greatly limits retail chains in capitalizing upon quantity discounts and other economic advantages of size. It has helped to maintain a system of small (although to a declining degree) and comparatively inefficient retailers instead of competition among several large, and presumably more efficient, retail chains.

Second, mergers among retailers have run into constant hostility from the Supreme Court, in, *e.g.*, both the leading Section 7 case[13] and the most radical recent antimerger one.[14]

Price Stability

The relationship between price stability, market structure and antitrust is close indeed. Economists in recent years have devised a number of theories to explain our constant post-war inflation, and agreement is most noticeable by its absence.[15] But whatever the reason, no one can dispute that cost-reduction in many industries, passed on to the consumer through lower prices, can do much to offset general inflation.

Antitrust is important here, both in encouraging cost-reducing innovations and in increasing the chance that they will be passed on to the consumer. Although there are differences of opinion, it is probably true that pure competition and oligopoly are better for cost-reduction than are monopolistic competition and monopoly. Thus, the effects of antitrust in replacing monopoly by oligopoly and in replacing concentrated by less concentrated oligopoly are significant here; so too, in reverse, would be any encouragement of monopolistic competition over oligopoly.

This structural effect also influences the possibility that cost-reduction will result in lower prices; the less the oligopolist's market share, the less power he has to retain the advantages of his cost-reduction for long. Important here also are the anti-collusive aspects of antitrust; collusive oligopolists are clearly better able to maintain prices than are non-collusive ones.

The above arguments refer to relative prices and assume a perpetual series of possible price reductions. But it is also important to notice that the more competitive an industry, the less power the seller has over price and the lower prices can be expected to be. Although an antitrust-caused change in market structure would thus lead to lower prices, it would not have the same repetitive effects of the previously discussed price-reducing pressures. The reduction would be a one-shot, structural affair, with inflationary percentages then figured on a lower basis.

A special aspect of this problem is the greater price flexibility of more competitive market structures. While this leads to lower prices in bad times, it causes higher ones in good times. This is a leading characteristic of agricultural markets.[16]

Economic Growth

Market structure, antitrust and economic growth are also closely intertwined. To some degree this parallels the argument above on price stability; cost-reductions release productive factors for other employment.

But the main connection among them lies in the deep and constant dispute over the relationship of market structure, research and new investment. High profits frequently characterize oligopoly and monopoly; are such profits necessary to finance and encourage progress? Must the innovator be protected against immediate competition, to obtain the benefits of his innovation and to make it worth his while to change? Do immediate price reductions, following from innovations as discussed above, discourage innovation? Related to this argument is the alleged advantage of giant corporations in conducting and financing modern research.

Some of the leading economists in the world have debated these matters for decades; we will not settle them here. Interested readers should consult the works of Joseph Schumpeter,[17] and of his present followers, such as the Harvard economist, John Kenneth Galbraith,[18] and the lawyer, Adolf Berle.[19] Sources for the opposing view are less easily specified, since it represents the majority school of American economists and its arguments are thus more often assumed than stated. Most economic texts present this customary view, as well as summarizing the Schumpeterian arguments.[20]

Employment

Antitrust and market structure are less closely related to employment than to price stability and economic growth, but the connection nevertheless exists. To some degree it may even be contrary— the resources released by cost-reducing innovations, as discussed above, may be human and may not be re-employed.[21]

Beyond this possible adverse relationship, the main connection lies through market structure's effect on the level of output: monopolies, monopolistic competition, and, much less decidedly, oligopolies restrict output and thus lessen employment. Is this effect major? The question has never been answered, and the relevant studies indicate it may be much less important than was formerly thought.[22]

Other Economic Goals

One possible national economic goal, economic efficiency, is discussed in a separate section below. Two other objectives, however—

ending or moderating the business cycle and changing the income distribution—must also be considered.

The relationship of market structure, the business cycle and antitrust is close but unclear. Schumpeter ascribes business cycles, in large part, to the effects of innovation;[23] thus the effect of antitrust upon innovation would be very important here. Most economists acknowledge the key part played by investment changes in the business cycle,[24] and investment depends in large part upon innovations and inventions. Even advocates of the "sunspot" theory of the business cycle[25] can claim a connection, since it operates through agriculture, the bastion of pure competition.

We come now to what is usually considered the main connection in this area, one related to much modern economic theory. The greater price flexibility of more competitive industries, as discussed above, would seem to aid in shortening depressions, making them self-corrective. A general decline in demand, like a limited one, would reduce prices and thus encourage in turn demand. This runs parallel to the traditional lower-wage cure for unemployment.

The stability of both prices and wages in the face of depression casts doubt upon the practical usefulness of this method for combating depression, but theoretically does not destroy the greater desirability of the more competitive market structures for this purpose. More moderately, and more practically, it may be that the success of antitrust in increasing the competitiveness of the economy, over what it would have been in its absence, may cause prices to be more flexible in a depression than would otherwise be the case.

The influence of antitrust on income distribution is closely related to the profit question. Despite the widows and orphans who traditionally receive dividends, one may shrewdly suspect that the rich are not deprived of them completely. To the degree that antitrust reduces profits by lowering prices and increasing output, it may cause an income redistribution from the richer to the poorer, and from the return to capital and the entrepreneur to the return to labor. Whether or not this is desirable is a political and perhaps ethical question, but not an economic one.

ECONOMISTS VERSUS LAWYERS
IN ANTITRUST

Much has been written about the divergences between lawyers and economists in antitrust.[26] A prominent legal authority has hailed with delight the ten-to-one ratio between lawyers and economists in antitrust enforcement;[27] Schumpeter once commented that his faith in the application of economic theory to economic problems grew dim when he reflected that such theory must be filtered through the legal mind.[28] When the generals display such distrust, what can be expected from the ranks?

This divergence shows itself in many ways. Terminology itself differs between the two professions—for example, "price discrimination" [29] and even "monopoly" [30] have different meanings for lawyers and economists. It is only human to assume that the large fees involved add their share to creating the mutual suspicion.

The author is fortunately saved from this battle by the fact that he is both an economist and a lawyer (listed alphabetically). But he cannot carry water on both shoulders. The above section on antitrust and national economic objectives is written purely from an economic viewpoint; in the subsequent sections on the antitrust laws, the "rule of reason" and *per se* violations require a legal viewpoint.

The differences explain the problem. How can a section on national economic objectives be written from a legal viewpoint? It would start with an examination of the legislatively declared objectives of the antitrust laws (completely ignored), go on to a consideration of the congressional debate and reports accompanying the statutes (completely ignored), and conclude with a survey of cases won and lost as an indication of success (also completely ignored).

If the legislative, "rule of reason" and *per se* sections were written from an economic viewpoint, they would divide legislation not by Act of Congress, but by the business practice or the type of market structure concerned. The use of economic evidence, rather than the use of affirmative defenses, would become the important dividing line between *per se* and "rule of reason" violations.

In this approach the courts, far from being the final judges, as, legally, they are, would become questionable participants whose

every decision would be analyzed by standards which judges are
not trained to understand. The operation of the laws, instead of
dividing business conduct into the legal and the illegal, would
divide it between the economically sound and unsound.

Is this conflict resolvable? From the viewpoint of personal interest
and conflicting knowledge, probably not. But the situation could
certainly be improved.

A parallel situation exists in the field of the law concerning insanity. No one can dispute that the question of what degree insanity
excuses crime is a general question, going far beyond medicine and
requiring an essentially political answer expressed through the law.
However, the questions of what constitutes insanity and of understanding its effects are medical.

Similarly, the degree to which restraints of trade are legal is a
political question, resolved through legislation and the law. But the
questions of what constitutes restraints of trade, and of what the
effects of various restraints may be, are economic questions, resolvable correctly only through economic theory and research.

ANTITRUST LEGISLATION

There are three major antitrust laws, the Sherman Act of 1890,
the Clayton Act of 1914 and the Federal Trade Commission Act
of 1914. Their original provisions, amendments and judicial interpretations form the substance of our antitrust laws.

The Sherman Act of 1890 is set in sweeping terms indeed. According to Section 1:

Every contract, combination in the form of trust or otherwise, or conspiracy, in restraint of trade or commerce among the several states, or
with foreign nations, is declared to be illegal.

What could be more inclusive than "every"? Section 2, affecting
"every person," seems equally all-inclusive:

Every person who shall monopolize, or attempt to monopolize, or com-
bine or conspire with any other person or persons, to monopolize any
part of the trade or commerce among the several states, or with foreign
nations, shall be deemed guilty of a misdemeanor.

With "any part" added to "every," subsequent legislation would appear superfluous and loopholes non-existent. But common sense should be applied to the statutory terminology. If taken too literally, these provisions would outlaw all interstate commerce—for every contract is in restraint of trade. The oral contract under which the reader bought this book is itself in restraint of trade. After its completion it prevents an identical trade between the buyer and another bookstore. But such a "restraint" (or, at least, the sale causing it) is the purpose of business.

Put so broadly, a dividing line would be hard to find. But the Sherman Act was not passed in a void. It was passed with the knowledge of centuries of developing law on restraints of trade in the United States and Great Britain. Such law applied to the act, as the common law applies to every American statute when relevant.

The Clayton Act of 1914 is as specific as the Sherman Act is general. Section 2 prohibits some forms of price discrimination, Section 3 outlaws some forms of exclusive salesmanship and Section 7 limits the legality of mergers.

Major antitrust legislation since 1914 has taken the form of amendments to the Clayton Act. Two such amendments are of sufficient importance to be frequently considered as separate legislation. The Robinson-Patman Act of 1936 strengthened greatly the Section 2 restrictions on price discrimination, and the Celler-Kefauver Act of 1950 removed some of the loopholes from the merger provisions of Section 7.

The Federal Trade Commission Act of 1914 is much broader in its provisions than the Clayton Act, both in the generality of its language and in its applicability to fields far beyond antitrust. The Act attempts to limit "unfair competition," whether or not related to antitrust. Section 5 of the Act declares:

Unfair methods of competition in commerce, and unfair or deceptive acts or practices in commerce, are declared unlawful.

At first glance it might be thought that such a provision is hostile to the whole spirit of antitrust; not the fairness but the effectiveness of competition concerns antitrust. And in the battle between "hard" and "soft" competition, as discussed below, this would seem to place Section 5 squarely on the side of "soft" competition. Indeed, the whole concept of "fair" competition—that is, of business relations conducted politely among gentlemen—has been much more highly developed in economies with no antitrust tradition, such as pre-war Germany,[31] than it has ever been in the United States.

But the division between antitrust and fair competition has not proved a serious problem in this country. Rather, Section 5 has become an integral part of our antitrust program. It has, first, been held to give the Federal Trade Commission jurisdiction over matters which would otherwise violate the Sherman Act.[32] And, second, it has been construed to give the FTC jurisdiction over such acts in their "incipiency," that is, before they are sufficiently developed to come within the scope of the Sherman Act.[33]

In addition to these major antitrust provisions, there are a host of more minor ones. The McGuire Act of 1952 exempts from antitrust provisions any state Fair Trade law giving a manufacturer the right to control the prices set by his retailers for his goods. The patent and copyright laws, based squarely on specific constitutional authorization,[34] protect industrial and creative contributions from immediate and direct competition. The federally regulated industries—railroads, television, interstate power and so forth—all have their own degree of antitrust exemption or coverage.[35] Labor unions enjoy a very controversial exemption,[36] while other pressure groups have acquired their own special rights—export associations, insurance companies, agricultural cooperatives, and so forth.[37]

ENFORCEMENT

Enforcement of the antitrust laws is shared among the Antitrust Division of the Department of Justice (an agent of the Executive, i.e., of the President), the Federal Trade Commission (an independent agency headed by bipartisan commissioners not removable by the President without cause), and private litigants. In addition, some states maintain active antitrust programs for their intrastate commerce.[38]

With so many cooks, disputed recipes are probably unavoidable. The Department of Justice and the FTC have concurrent jurisdiction under the Clayton Act; the Sherman Act was originally enforced by the Justice Department alone. But the broad interpretation given to Section 5 of the FTC Act, as discussed above, has

created an effective joint jurisdiction over much Sherman Act subject matter as well. Private litigants, spurred on by the triple damages permitted under antitrust legislation (three times the actual
damage suffered), can sue under almost every antitrust provision.

But the cuisine war, if it is permissible to speak so of the august
cooks involved, has been avoided in part by the strict rationing involved. As Mr. Simon makes clear (Article 9) both the Antitrust
Division and the FTC are so short of personnel that neither has
reason to interfere with the other's suits. Over both, as the final
arbiters, brood the courts and, as the last resort, the Supreme Court.

The Supreme Court, indeed, plays a much more important role
in antitrust cases than in most judicial areas. The hierarchy of appeal lies not from a district court to a court of appeals, but directly
to the Supreme Court. If the Supreme Court refuses to review, there
is no review available at all, a consideration which leads the highest
court to hear a very large proportion of antitrust cases.[39]

The Supreme Court itself has pointed out the drawbacks and has
expressed the hope that Congress will amend the law.[40] Of all cases,
antitrust ones, with their voluminous records, intricate issues and
widespread effects are most in need of the careful and laborious
review which the Supreme Court does not have the time to grant.

The above procedure applies only to suits brought by the Department of Justice. FTC cases, under the normal administrative procedure, are tried first by the FTC, appealed to a court of appeals
and, only then, appealed to the Supreme Court.[41] And, as Mr. Simon
points out (Article 9), cases won by the defendants before a court
of appeals cannot be taken to the Supreme Court without the
Solicitor-General's hard-to-come-by consent.

THE RULE OF REASON

One of the leading issues of antitrust is the constant battle between advocates of a "rule of reason" standard in antitrust cases
and advocates of a broadly applied *per se* standard. But before the
issue is examined, it is necessary to define our terms.

Although the "rule of reason" is always stated in the singular, and
therefore is so used in this essay, there are actually three different
"rules of reason."

(1) The Ancillary Rule

First, there is the traditional common law meaning of the term, the so-called ancillary rule. A restraint of trade is legal under this rule of reason if it is only ancillary (subordinate and, in effect, necessary) to an otherwise legitimate business agreement. An example is the sale of a business or of a professional practice under a contract providing that the seller will not compete with the buyer. Presumably, no sale would be possible if the professional or businessman concerned could open up next door after the sale and win back his patients or customers.

If such an agreement were not legal, it would greatly impede the mobility of business ownership and of entrepreneurial and professional talent. Since considerable mobility is a prime prerequisite of our capitalist system, such contracts in restraint of trade (and what contract could be more in restraint of trade?) are perfectly legal under this rule of reason.

But they are legal only to the extent that they are genuinely necessary to the contract. Thus they are limited in both time and space. A New York physician, selling his practice on Park Avenue, could not validly agree not to resume practice for fifty years in New York, or for any time at all in California. Such an agreement would restrain competition without protecting the New York buyer.[42]

The ancillary rule, where it is applied in antitrust, is usually in the context of considering the beneficial results of a sale, and thus falls under the third definition of the rule of reason, as discussed below. Its one direct application, outside franchising, may be to the failing company defense, which permits a business in poor financial condition to merge even if it would otherwise violate Section 7 of the Clayton Act.[43] Here the sale might be considered ancillary to the primary interest of salvaging the endangered assets.

(2) Action Judged by Its Effects

The second, most widely applicable meaning of the rule of reason is that originally laid down by the Supreme Court in the 1911 *Standard Oil* case, as follows:

[Reason is] the measure used for the purpose of determining whether in a given case a particular act had or had not brought about the wrong against which the statute provided.[44]

The *Standard Oil* case read such a rule of reason into the Sherman Act. However, the statutory language of the Clayton Act directly embraces the concept that specific acts are illegal only if they result in certain harmful effects.

(3) Balancing Contrasting Effects

Finally, there is a third, much more intricate, meaning of the rule of reason. This formulation requires a court to balance adverse and favorable results of a particular act in order to judge its legality. For example, suppose two weak, but still surviving firms merge in order to compete more effectively against some more successful rival. Does this lessen or increase competition? Does it tend toward or away from monopoly? One less corporation is competing in the industry, but the merged firm is presumably competing more effectively. Only a thorough economic analysis can resolve this question, and even then no one would be sure of the correct resolution.

Most business acts are not so simple in their effects as is assumed under the first and second meanings of the rule of reason. Certainly a high proportion must result in these diverse and hard to judge effects. Thus this balancing action has received the occasional endorsement of the Supreme Court.[45] The particular argument that a merger may strengthen competition against a larger competitor has been endorsed specifically by the Supreme Court,[46] by the Justice Department in approving certain mergers (for example, the Kaiser-Willys merger[47]), by a congressional committee which drafted the revised Section 7,[48] and, of course, by defendants in Section 7 cases.[49]

Contrasting the Meanings

But despite the clear logic underlying the approach, it has aroused a host of enemies.[50] Nor is this surprising. Antitrust cases are notoriously long and complex. One antitrust economist, for example, who worked on a case for two years and then published a book about it, admitted he had not read the whole record.[51] Indeed, who could? In the face of such long, expensive and uncertain judicial contests, can anything justify even greater length, expense and uncertainty?

Put that way, the answer would seem to be no. Better a simplified rule of reason than cases which outlive the personnel involved in them. The old judicial joke about the lawyer who gives his lawyer son-in-law a will case as a dowry could be applied to antitrust without trouble. But appealing as such a solution may be, it is fallacious on at least two grounds.

First, if it is assumed that a balancing rule of reason reflects much better the realities of the business world than a more simplified one, then long drawn out cases would be more beneficial than ones decided by a too simplified approach. Second, and more practically, antitrust cases at present contain many issues that could be removed or simplified, thus giving time for a sophisticated rule of reason. For example, much time is presently spent on the issues of the relevant markets and lines of commerce—that is, what industry and product definitions should be followed? Such issues can have great practical implications, but are of far less importance than the effects of the challenged act itself. If simplified rules must be applied, why not in these areas? Fortunately, the Supreme Court has shown some recent impatience with these endless wrangles.[52]

But whatever rule of reason is followed, the first and most basic issue in antitrust policy is whether any rule of reason standard should be used, and if so, in which cases? The advocates of stronger antitrust policies greatly favor the application of *per se* standards.

PER SE *VIOLATIONS*

According to Mr. Justice Black, speaking for the Supreme Court:

. . . there are certain agreements or practices which because of their *pernicious effect on competition* and *lack of any redeeming virtue* are conclusively presumed to be unreasonable and therefore illegal without elaborate inquiry as to the precise harm they have caused or the business excuse for their use.[53] (italics added)

The first italicized phrase is the second definition of the rule of reason; the second italicized phrase is the third definition; the whole paragraph taken together rules out both definitions in certain cases.

Specific Per Se *Offenses*

There are four generally accepted *per se* violations today, all under Section 1 of the Sherman Act; according to Professor Markham (Article 3), "horizontal" mergers under Section 7 of the Clayton Act also today belong in this category. The four Sherman Act violations are price-fixing (both "horizontal," i.e., between competitors, and "vertical," i.e., between a firm and a supplier, distributor or retailer); group boycotts; market division (between competitors but not, today, between a firm and its distributors, suppliers or retailers); and tie-in sales, that is, requiring a customer to buy a second good or service as a condition of buying the one he wants.[54]

What do these four business practices have in common? According to Mr. Justice Black, as quoted above, they lack any "redeeming virtue" or any doubt as to their "pernicious effects." If this is so, the rule of reason is not so much set aside as applied and found inapplicable. More precisely, the time of the courts is saved by a judicial ruling, in advance of the trial, on what would be inevitably shown if trial on those issues were allowed.

Logical Bases

But life is seldom so simple and defendants are uniformly opposed to *per se* rules. Mr. Justice Black's definition, as given above, is too sweeping. The most that can be said is that the great majority of *per se* offenses could not be defended under a rule of reason approach. For example, it could well be that a price-fixing agreement between two small firms might save them from mutual extermination, a fate which could benefit only their competitors, some of whom might be considerably larger and more anti-competitive than they are.

We are faced at the outset with an unanswered factual question —how important are such exceptions? There is no way to tell; present *per se* offenses have been so almost since the beginning of an

active federal antitrust program or, at the least, before there was
time to have a number of cases involving such offenses tried on their
merits under a rule of reason.

But there is one possible *per se* category—Professor Markham's
suggested area of horizontal mergers—which was considered on the
merits in the past. Here the record is plain. As Mr. Simon makes
clear (Article 9), cases before district courts and courts of appeal have been closely argued and decided both ways. Thus in
this area, certainly, no evidence exists that a *per se* rule would simply
reach the same results as a rule of reason standard with considerable
savings of time and money.

The traditional *per se* offenses—horizontal and vertical price
fixing, group boycotts, horizontal market divisions and tie-in sales
—are uniformly condemned by traditional economic theory. Nor
has this condemnation been affected by the Keynesian Revolution
of the past third of a century, for that Revolution is not concerned
with this area of economics. But it has been affected by what might
be called the Counter-Keynesian Revolution.

Standing at the fore of this Counter-Revolution is the Department
of Economics of the University of Chicago, whose most prominent
member, Milton Friedman, a Goldwater economic adviser in 1964,
is one of the best American economists. Professor Friedman has not
himself done much work in antitrust theory, although his reminders
of the large role of government in promoting monopoly in the United
States[55] deserve more widespread acknowledgment.

But Professor Lester Telser, also of the University of Chicago, has
been challenging in economic theory the presumed evil of some of
these *per se* practices, especially of tie-in sales, following in the
tradition of the University of Chicago Law School.[56]

Despite this intellectual challenge, however, it seems safe to say
that the traditional *per se* offenses do stand condemned by both
traditional economic theory and the great mass of interested antitrust economists and experts. Indeed, it would be hard to find a
reputable defender in academic circles of the McGuire Act, which
upholds state Fair Trade laws as described above. Supporters of a
more moderate antitrust policy frequently prove their general ortho-
doxy by the vigor of their attacks on these pernicious evils.[57]

Because of this near unanimity of informed opinion, the issue of
the rule of reason versus a *per se* approach is important in con-

sidering whether the *per se* approach will be applied more widely than it is at present—not in considering whether it will continue dominant in its present domain.

Loopholes

There is a tendency of the courts to uphold otherwise *per se* violations, when they wish to do so, not by finding an exception but by denying that the alleged offense fits the condemned category at all. This is human but hardly intellectually defensible. Two important Supreme Court cases illustrate this application.[58]

Some lower courts, in upholding what would appear to be *per se* violations, have been more open with their reasons. A district court in Pennsylvania, for example, upheld a tie-in contract involving community antennae and service for such antennae on the ground that the goods and service were both new and experimental and that to allow outside service by firms without experience in the field (and no other firm had any experience in that sort of work) would wreck both the antennae and the defendant's reputation.

Upholding a *per se* violation on so specific a ground does not present the same danger to the future of the *per se* rule as would upholding one on a less precise ground. The Pennsylvania court specifically restricted the legality of the tie-in sale to the period of time when this new industry was still experimental.[59]

Practical Importance

It should not be thought that the application of a *per se* rule either dooms the defendant to lose the case or removes from the plaintiff a heavy burden of proof. The plaintiff's case can be the same under the *per se* rule as under the rule of reason. The main difference is that the defendant cannot raise any affirmative defenses justifying his course of action.

To some degree this is simply a question of words. At the most, it must be determined whether the plaintiff or the defendant must bear the burden of proof. For example, examine the two following ways of stating a *per se* rule:

1. All tie-in sales involving a certain minimum of interstate commerce are illegal.

2. All tie-in sales not involving a new product and its service and involving a certain minimum of interstate commerce are illegal.

Both are *per se* rules and neither permits a rule of reason approach. Yet one permits the Pennsylvania exception discussed above and the other does not. Is there, therefore, such a great difference between *per se* and rule of reason standards? Or examine, for example, the following two possible formulations of the law:

1. All tie-in sales not involving a new product and its service and involving a certain minimum of interstate commerce are illegal.
2. All tie-in sales involving a certain minimum of interstate commerce are illegal unless the defendant can justify them as involving a new product and its service.

Both 1 and 2 state the same law; 1 is a *per se* statement and 2 a rule of reason statement. The only difference, although a most important one legally, is that under statement 1 the plaintiff bears the burden of proof as to the nonexistence of a new product and service, and that under statement 2 the burden falls on the defendant as to their existence.

NATURE OF THE COMPETITION WHICH ANTITRUST SHOULD PROMOTE

Professor Dewey expresses the view (Article 2) that all antitrust cases can be viewed as part of a judicial search for a usable definition of competition. He also concludes, in effect, that the search has not so far been noteworthy for its success.

If this is so, it casts a peculiar light indeed on our antitrust laws. If there is one generally undisputed conclusion in antitrust—from (until recently) the Supreme Court itself,[60] to the expert commentators,[61] to the politicians who passed the necessary legislation[62]—it is that the purpose of our antitrust policy is to promote competition in the American economy. Foreign observers, indeed, have frequently noted the prevalence of competition as a unique feature of the American economy.[63] How perplexing it would be if all this concerted effort to promote competition were handicapped by lack of knowledge and agreement as to what constitutes competition.

Yet it must be admitted that this is an area in which economic theory does not speak clearly. In traditional economic theory, competition was identified with pure competition. That pure competition is not very typical of the American economy requires no great knowledge of economics to be realized.

Active Versus Passive Competition

Pure competition implies no active competition among different producers. Each firm is so small that one cannot affect another; thus, no farmer believes that the amount of wheat his neighbor grows will have much to do with the price he himself will receive for his own wheat. This "passive" competition—where each producer competes with all other producers in the mass, but with none individually—is very different indeed from the active, personal competition which most Americans, and especially most American businessmen, think of when they think of acting competitively. But which version is it the purpose of the antitrust laws to promote?

First, active competition, among companies with large enough market shares to affect each other, goes together with substantial *market power*—the power of each seller to set its own prices without losing all its customers, even if it sets them higher than the prices charged by its competitors. But it is just this market power which is considered by many antitrust experts to be the primary foe of antitrust policy.

Professors Carl Kaysen and Donald Turner (Article 5) base their program for breaking up giant corporations, as analyzed by Professor Whitney (Article 6), squarely upon the market power of the corporations to be dissolved, although they base estimates of that market power on the size of the market shares.[64]

Here we have come to one of the fundamental issues of antitrust policy. Market power, derived from a substantial market share, is the traditional enemy of the advocates of competition. It is that market power which enables firms to raise prices and profits, reduce output and distort resources in the traditional manner of evil monopoly. But what is to be done when the benefits of active competition depend on that very market power?

The question arises whether there is some intermediate business size which could maintain the giant corporations' advantages in research and economic progress while minimizing their power over price. How large must a corporation be, in absolute size and in market share, to take advantage of research opportunities? Could it be small enough, at least in large industries, to permit many competitors and at least a diluted oligopoly? [65] New research along these lines would seem very desirable today.

What kind of competition do the courts look for as evidence favorable to defendants? The author has read the records of most of the Celler-Kefauver cases, and it is primarily evidence of active competition which is introduced there. In the first Supreme Court case, for example, involving a conglomerate merger (one in which the merged firms had no direct business relationship before the merger), the defendant (Consolidated Foods) submitted to the Supreme Court a lengthy brief listing the diverse and, indeed, overwhelming evidence introduced in the lower courts on active competition in the dehydrated onion and garlic industries.[66] According to Consolidated Foods, the law of the jungle was peace itself compared to the bitter rivalry in the sale of dehydrated onions and garlic.

Most antitrust violations assume a market structure other than pure competition. Price-fixing, market division, group boycotts and tie-in sales would all be impossible (except on an industry-wide basis) under pure competition where no firm can directly affect another. How, indeed, could anyone introduce any evidence as to passive competition? Only through evidence on market structure, as discussed above.

"Hard" versus "Soft" Competition

As discussed above, American law includes the concepts of "fair" and "unfair" competition. Closely paralleling this division (although both are presumably handled legally and are thus "fair") is the division between "hard" and "soft" competition.

Much of the business action which led to public demand for the antitrust laws was hard as could be conceived of; indeed, much of it would now be illegal. The price wars, price rebates, railroad discrimination and other techniques with which Standard Oil, for example, won control of the oil industry, were the very hard competitive techniques which antitrust advocates might have been thought to have always advocated. If competition is "good," why is not more competition, or harder competition, better?

This problem lies unresolved behind many an antitrust dispute. No doubt, each small businessman and exploited consumer who demanded the original antitrust legislation would have been very happy to have outlawed monopoly practices among his suppliers or in the stores where he shopped while legalizing them for himself or his customers, and his competitors. For, whatever the theoretical advantages of competition, the advantage of risking one's livelihood is not apparent to most people.

Much modern economic theory has developed around the laws of probability.[67] While somewhat esoteric for this essay, one aspect is directly relevant. Which is preferable: a 100 per cent chance of a 6 per cent profit, or a 50 per cent chance of a 12 per cent profit and a 50 per cent chance of zero profit or worse? A 100 per cent chance of a 6 per cent profit or a 60 per cent chance of a 12 per cent profit and a 40 per cent chance of zero profit or worse? A 100 per cent chance of a 6 per cent profit or a 40 per cent chance of a 12 per cent profit and 60 per cent of zero profit or worse?

Of course, the answer will differ according to the attitude of each of us to risk. But to anyone who prefers safety, collusive actions are highly to be desired. Adam Smith, in his famous remark that competitors could not gather in a room without conspiring in restraint of trade,[68] assumed that every businessman preferred safety. But Adam Smith was a college professor, a member of a profession known to prefer safety to risk in regard to income.

While it is impossible to draw an absolute line between soft and hard competition, a logical division would be between actions which only threaten competitors' profit levels, and those which threaten their business existence. Assuming such conduct to be reciprocal, many businessmen clearly prefer soft competition.

It can be argued that the Standard Oil practices are condemned not because they ruined competitors, but because they ended competition in the oil industry. This is so, and competitive acts which end competition can hardly be justified, even by advocates of the hardest competition. But as long as entry into the industry is easy, new firms could always enter to replace the ruined ones,[69] and as long as this is so, the hardest competition could be justified. Only where the winning competitor gains sufficient power to prevent entry would such practices stand condemned even by advocates of hard competition.

Competition versus Competitors

Closely related to the issue of hard versus soft competition is the issue of whether it is the primary purpose of the antitrust laws to promote competition or to protect competitors.

Until recently, it would not have been admitted that this was a real issue. As Professor Markham makes clear (Article 3) the Supreme Court, in the prominent *Brown Shoe* case, hastened to insist that its object was the protection of competition, even while deciding the case on the basis of protecting competitors.[70]

More forthrightness, or less guile, has marked recent Supreme Court decisions. In a 1966 case, it completely ignored the great number of new entrants into the Los Angeles retail grocery industry.[71] Instead, it concentrated on one factor alone—the number of firms which had left the industry in recent years.[72] This fact alone, coupled with the decline in total number, was held sufficient to make the merger between two retail grocery chains illegal.[73] Thus, as clearly as possible, the Supreme Court has set the preservation of competitors over the protection of competition as the primary goal of our antitrust laws.

Such a standard, if carried to the point of protecting every individual competitor, would make every merger illegal. Is there any basis for such a standard?

Such protection may really fulfill the desires of the small businessmen who originally fought for antitrust legislation with teeth in it. Who can doubt that they would have preferred to have been individually protected? Why then does the "number of competitors standard" arouse such expert opposition?

Partly, it results from the Supreme Court's not taking in to account the fact that withdrawals from an industry, accompanied by frequent but fewer entrants, is often a characteristic of an industry growing in efficiency and maturity. Thus such a standard could be anti-efficient, setting the antitrust laws in opposition to efficiency in our economy. This aspect of the problem, an extremely significant one, is discussed further below.

How to Measure Competition

In view of the different views on what constitutes competition, it is not surprising that a similar lack of agreement exists on how to estimate the competitiveness of an industry. Broadly speaking, there are three main approaches: (1) structure (is the market characterized by purely competitive, oligopolistic, monopolistic or monopolistically competitive features?); (2) conduct (how do the firms in the industry set their prices and output, handle their advertising, and so forth?); and (3) performance (how does the industry compare with others in profitability, growth, product improvement and so on?). The English courts, as Mr. Leyland recounts their standards (Article 10), use all three.

Within each group there are many different approaches and no general agreement as to what particular tests prove. Generally speaking, advocates of strong antitrust policy favor structural tests, since these are more likely than the others to show a lack of a desirable level of competition, the American economy being more competitive in conduct and performance than in structure. Structural tests also have the advantage, from this viewpoint, of being easier to apply and of approaching the speed and simplicity of *per se* rules.

Structural Tests of Competition

The easiest structural test of competition is the *concentration ratio* in an industry, the operation of market share held by the leading two, three, four or some other small number of firms. Since this approach is thoroughly explored by Professor Adelman (Article 1), there is no need to review it here.

The most widely accepted structural test is ease of entry into an industry. If there are no barriers to entry to prevent new competitors whenever an industry tends toward monopoly profits or inefficient performance, antitrust violations tend to be self-corrective. Such a test is accepted among economists,[74] defendants,[75] and even, at times, by the Supreme Court.[76]

An ease of entry test is not easy, however, to apply. Wide differences exist in any particular case where the issue is raised as to how easy in fact entry is. In some cases it is hard to believe that plaintiff and defendant are referring to the same industry. Even such simple factual matters as how many new entrants were received into the particular industry are disputed.[77] Nor is this surprising. Who is to say if a firm which produces only part of a product line, or a corporate reorganization, or even a conglomerate merger, represents entry?

A number-of-competitors test can also be tried, along with a similar test, whether the number of competitors is growing or declining. Although subject to some difficulties when defining which firms are in the particular market concerned (see Article 1), such an approach is usually not too difficult to formulate. But its lack of logic, separate from market shares, seems clear.

Conduct Tests of Competition

The practical nature of conduct standards recommend them to many defendants and their lawyers, as well as to those who believe that many industries, structurally noncompetitive, can rate as competitive in regard to what actually takes place within them and among their firms.

One conduct test is the independence of rival firms. The presence or absence of interlocking directories (an area where the present law is weak), might rank as a structural test of conduct. The courts have been hostile to practices which could lead to such interlocking directories, as, for example, the purchase of corporate shares by a rival.[78] Independence among rival firms is frequently argued in terms of whether the firms concerned have in the past been convicted of violating Section 1 of the Sherman Act, since price-fixing is the clearest sign of lack of independent action.[79]

Also important in regard to independence is whether the industry is characterized by price leadership, that is, one firm initiating price changes and its competitors following. Where such price leadership exists, independence is certainly severely limited. The steel industry, in the past, was well known for this price pattern and, although in the far past steel won a major antitrust case,[80] its recent record in the courts has not been in its interests.[81]

The presence or absence of price rigidity—that is, the frequency with which firms change their prices to reflect changed market conditions—is also an important conduct test.[82] It is widely thought that oligopolies are characterized by price rigidity, supposedly one of their main disadvantages.[83] Empirical evidence exists that oligopolies in fact show considerable price flexibility;[84] this, therefore, must be left an open question. Whatever the truth, evidence that particular firms do change their prices frequently would seem to be good evidence of competitive conduct.[85]

Price flexibility or rigidity faces, however, an important evidentiary problem. It is easy to show, through corporate records or the trade press, what list prices have been and how often they have changed. But are such list prices the real prices? Many industries indulge in price shading, and then the price is not the list price but list price minus a discount.[86] The real question is how frequently this latter price has changed, and for this there is much less empirical evidence, especially since much of it is deliberately secret.

Important to defendants in this context, as discussed above, is evidence on the active nature of their competitiveness. One firm placed in evidence the remark of a customer that one of its salesmen was so aggressive that he appeared in his actions somewhat similar to a Ku Klux Klan dragon in the old days in Oklahoma.[87] Could anyone be more aggressively competitive?

Such non-price competition, including not only aggressive salesmen but advertising, product improvement, easy credit terms and so forth, is important not only here but in the next category of judging an industry—economic performance. Defendants point to such non-price competition and argue that it can exist in the absence of the traditional price competition.[88] But the courts, although welcoming aggressive salesmanship, are generally not friendly to aggressive advertising. One judge even commented on the low level of television today as an unfortunate result of such techniques.[89]

Performance Tests of Competition

To those who believe that the function of federal legislation is neither to protect individuals nor to reflect the shifting power pattern of American interest groups, but to promote certain desirable national goals, performance tests of competition seem the most logical. After all, if competition is desired it is desired not because it is good as an end of itself but because it leads to certain worthwhile results. Perhaps, therefore, neither structural nor conduct tests are

as useful as the direct question, does the industry concerned perform
well economically? Do the challenged firms give us the economic
results we want from industry?

Profit plays a confused role in this area. Even the most extreme
antitrust advocate would presumably admit that management earn-
ing high profits is doing its job better than management making
mediocre or negative profits. Nevertheless, the presence of high
profits is sometimes used as a sign of unsatisfactory performance:
the presence in an *industry* of profits higher than necessary to
attract the needed capital, and higher than profits in more competitive industries, is the result of monopoly.

Such a connection is indisputable. Much more questionable is
hostility to profit based on hostility to those who receive them.
Whether or not higher returns to stockholders through higher
dividends or capital appreciation is desirable is not an economic but
a political and ethical question. It is not by itself an economic reason for viewing high profits with hostility.

Higher profits in a *firm*, rather than in an industry, compared to
other firms in the same industry rather than in other industries,
need show no such greater monopoly. It is possible that it may, as,
for example, when the largest firm in an industry makes the highest
profits of any firm in that particular industry. But it need not even
then—General Motors, the largest and most profitable automobile
firm, is generally considered the most efficient as well.[90] But in steel,
for example, the highest profits for years have gone to firms considerably smaller than U.S. Steel.[91]

The government,[92] and at times, the courts,[93] tend to treat such
high firm profits as signs of, if not bad performance, at least of
undesirable performance. In one aspect of the problem, this is
logical. High profits have long been cited by economists as a necessary prerequisite for rapid economic growth, as discussed above.
Certainly in merger cases, therefore, a merger by a highly profitable
firm, is at best unnecessary—the firm could presumably finance the
same growth internally out of its profits, or attract new capital by its
profit record.

Other performance tests are much less arguable in terms of
readily obtainable facts and figures. The contribution of a firm to
our national economic growth may be deduced from its own growth
rate, or from its record on new products and techniques of produc-

tion. But here again a firm with such a record could be expected to expand fully on its own, without needing the protection of special exceptions to the antitrust laws. Contributions to national goals such as high employment are even vaguer, while stable prices in a firm are hardly consistent with the antitrust goal of flexible prices. Of course, a record of always raising and never lowering prices might be considered as contrary to our anti-inflationary goal, but this aspect does not figure prominently in antitrust cases.

What Is Workable Competition?

Antitrust for several decades has been the home of a most illusive concept, usually designated as "workable competition." With pure competition certainly unobtainable and possibly undesirable, this academic substitute has won a horde of supporters. Its vagueness, as is often the case, has only increased its popularity.

Workable competition is based on the work of Columbia economist John Maurice Clark.[94] It has been authoritatively defined as having the following characteristics:

1. *Number of Effective Competitive Sellers:* . . . Absolute size has no significance . . . where firms are few in number, special study would usually be needed to determine whether an industry were workably competitive.
2. *Opportunity for Entry:* . . . relative freedom of entry . . . is a fundamental requisite for effective competition. . . . Without this condition, it is idle to expect effective competition.
3. *Independence of Rivals:* . . . each firm (must pursue) its own individual advantage.
4. *Predatory Preclusive Practices:* . . . There should be (none) . . . such that their natural effect would be to enable the user to eliminate rivals without regard to their efficiency. . . .
5. *Rate of Growth of the Industry or Market:* . . . [This is not] a direct economic indicator of the state of competition. . . . Rate of growth, however, is often important in determining the significance to be attached to other factors, and particularly to numbers and reasonable opportunity for entry.
6. *Character of Market Incentives to Competitive Moves:* . . . effective competition may hinge on the condition that the initiator of a competitive action can expect a gain. . . .
7. *Product Differentiation:* . . . Extreme product differentiation may

allow real positions of monopoly. . . . Relatively mild differentiation
. . . may be a factor favorable to the intensiveness of competition. . . .

8. *Meeting or Matching the Prices of Rivals:* . . . Meeting a rival's in-
   ducements is the means whereby competition diffuses the gains of
   productive efficiency.

9. *Excess Capacity:* . . . a moderate and varying amount of excess
   capacity naturally tends to develop . . . in response to the rise or
   fall of demand in a competitive industry . . . its presence is favorable to the effectiveness of competition, if other criteria of competition are present.

10. *Price Discrimination:* . . . Some types of price discrimination may
    stimulate effective competition; others may be evidence of effective
    monopoly. . . .[95]

Five of the above criteria—the importance of the number of
sellers, the opportunity for entry, the independence of rivals, the
absence of predatory preclusive practices, and meeting price
changes—are characteristics also of pure competition. A sixth, price
discrimination, is absent from pure competition, but cannot be cate-
gorized here since it can fall on either side of workable competition
standards. Another two—excess capacity and a high rate of growth—
may or may not exist in particular purely competitive industries as
they move from equilibrium to equilibrium.

But the remaining two—product differentiation and market rewards for competitive moves—are directly contrary to purely competitive characteristics. If these two characteristics are desirable,
then pure competition is not.

The issue may seem irrelevant to those who stop with the thought
that pure competition is unobtainable anyway. But that fact does
not prevent the courts from judging industries on the basis of how
closely they approximate pure competition.[96] But if product differentiation and rewards for competitive actions are desirable, pure
competition as a standard is clearly not.

The degree to which such standards reflect the American economy
obviously differs greatly from industry to industry. Further, the
question arises whether an industry can be workably competitive
if it does not have one of the more important of the characteristics.
An example is the automobile industry, which clearly has no ease of
entry, if it has any entry opportunity at all. Is the automobile in-

dustry workably competitive? It would seem to have many other competitive characteristics, and has often been though to be highly competitive by those who believe in active competition.[97] But what use are standards which are desirable but not necessary, since their presence or absence does not answer the question of whether an industry is workably competitive, unless they are all absent or all present?

Some of these criteria have strong judicial support. The number of sellers,[98] the opportunity for entry,[99] the independence of rivals,[100] the absence of preclusive practices,[101] and, possibly, the meeting of a rival's prices[102] (which raises the issue of price leadership), have all been judicially embraced. But some others are less popular. Product differentiation,[103] excess capacity,[104] and rewards to an innovator[105] have all been used to show the absence rather than the presence of competition.

The present status of workable competition can be defined as follows: there is no list of recognizable characteristics, and there is certainly no recognizable process, which will enable anyone to identify an industry as workably competitive. To that degree, "workable competition" is still a term in search of a definition. But the concept of workable competition does have a more pragmatic meaning, if it is defined as any industry the courts will accept as competitive.

EFFICIENCY AS AN ANTITRUST OBJECTIVE

Efficiency can be defined as a smoldering antitrust issue. It is not yet recognized as such by most observers, but stands ready as soon as it is so recognized to take its place as perhaps the most vital and controversial of all antitrust issues.

Is there, in fact, any division between efficiency and antitrust? The original supporters of antitrust probably assumed none, both because of the greater efficiency which traditional economic theory assigns to competitive markets, and because the trusts of the later nineteenth century had notoriously reached their advantageous positions by predatory rather than efficient means.[106]

From a criminal law and moral viewpoint, the efficiency of an antitrust violator is, of course, irrelevant. A father of ten could hardly defend the murder of one child on the ground that the remaining nine would have more to eat. It is not for a court to weigh the practical advantages of criminal actions, and violations under the original Sherman Act have criminal as well as civil penalties.

However, the mergers, price discrimination and exclusive practices regulated under the Clayton Act are overwhelmingly civil in nature. Further, they are business activities, as Professor Handler makes clear (Article 8), which have valid business justifications, including greater efficiency. That Congress recognized this factor is shown by the fact that, unlike the Sherman Act provisions, the Clayton Act provides for restricted application.

Is the greater efficiency which may result from what would otherwise be antitrust violations sufficient to make such alleged violations legal? Nothing in the statutes themselves say so, and the courts have been hesitant to consider efficiency as a factor to justify such violations.

Professor Dewey (Article 2) believes that, despite their general silence on the issue of efficiency, the courts have given it a high place in the hierarchy of reasons underlying their decisions. But Professor Dewey's examples are monopolization cases under Section 2 of the Sherman Act, and such cases are mostly taken from the distant past.[107] Can the same be said for more recent Clayton Act cases?

In one area, mergers, the Supreme Court has led the way, not only ignoring efficiency but repudiating it as an antitrust objective to be weighed with other factors in reaching decisions.[108] The assumption, and recently the *admitted* assumption, has thus shifted away from an interest in the greater efficiency of highly competitive markets to an interest in traditional competition, irrespective of efficiency.

But the nature of these recent cases was signally different from the traditional patterns of fact leading, in Professor Dewey's judgment, to judicial support of efficient firms. In the latter type of case, courts were faced with choosing between a giant corporation— for example, U.S. Steel[109]—and the smaller but still large corporations that would have arisen if the defendants had been dissolved. These decisions which favored the defendants have been widely attacked—and, in the author's view justifiably so—on the ground that the advantages of size accrue more to moderate than to giant corporations.[110] This point has been discussed more fully above.

Certainly, small steel companies have been run more efficiently than U.S. Steel.[111] Indeed, one of these more efficient companies, Bethlehem Steel, lost a merger case in which the efficiency argument was raised partly on the ground that it operated so efficiently without the claimed advantages of the challenged Youngstown merger.[112]

But the Supreme Court, in its relevant recent Section 7 cases, was faced by no such choice between dinosaurs and elephants. Rather, it had to choose between minnows and tadpoles. Challenged mergers have concerned retailing and involved firms small in absolute size and market share.[113]

Although the Court seemed unaware of the fact, the basic nature of the choice, in economic terms, had shifted greatly. No longer was the choice a simple one between monopoly or oligopoly, concentrated oligopoly or less concentrated oligopoly. Rather, the choice was one between monopolistic competition and some very slightly concentrated form of oligopoly, and the Supreme Court chose the former.

This view is recent, and has enjoyed a sharp and penetrating minority position.[114] We cannot tell to what degree it speaks for the future. But if it does, how significant is such opposition to efficiency likely to prove?

Several observations are necessary here. First, the economic meaning of efficiency is by no means completely clear. Traditionally, efficiency in economics meant the most productive allocation of resources among different industries (a factor under which pure competition was more efficient than monopoly), and criteria less generally agreed on—the best allocation of goods among consumers, the production of the right goods and the use of the least expensive methods of production.[115]

Thus traditional economic efficiency is a concept based on cost minimization—or on production maximization with given costs. By this standard, monopolistic competition is highly inefficient and the Supreme Court majority view could have drastic and unfortunate results. But it is not the only standard.

The importance of traditional efficiency has recently been severely challenged in the pages of the *American Economic Review*, the journal of the American Economic Association, the professional economic society. According to this study, other forms of cost minimization and production increase are of far greater importance. Worker motivation, the correct interplay of production techniques, and so forth, play a much greater role here than the cheapest way of using inputs.[116] And, although the matter is so far unexplored, it is possible that the greater diffusion of owner-management under monopolistic competition might cause a higher level of this type of efficiency under that market structure.[117]

The point must be raised (preferably before the Supreme Court)[118] that hostility to efficiency runs counter to our congressionally-declared, national economic goals—indeed, to all three of them. More efficient firms contribute more to economic growth and (other things being equal) to employment, while cheaper methods of production passed on to the consumer are the best barrier against inflation. If the antitrust laws are used to favor inefficiency, what will become of these national objectives? In any event, the legal position is clear. With much antitrust legislation predating these national objectives, and with no later antitrust legislation overtly contradicting them, the courts are theoretically bound to consider them in any case where they are applicable.[119]

Schumpeterian efficiency (innovation), was not directly involved in the recent Section 7 retailing cases, such enterprise apparently characterizing retailers of many different sizes, and the relevant industries.[120]

Does the majority Supreme Court view imply judicial hostility to this type of efficiency? There is no logical difference in the cases to distinguish these situations and the modern Court has shown a consistent hostility to size as such.[121]

To summarize, there are at least two reasons to assume that the present clash between antitrust and efficiency may become an important and divisive national issue should it continue and become better known. First, there is the popular American devotion to efficiency which would tend to put popular opinion in opposition to the present Supreme Court position.[122] And, second, there is the clash between such a view and the national economic goals of price stability, economic growth and high employment as specified by congressional legislation.

CONCLUSIONS

There is not room to consider many other important antitrust issues—the degree to which antitrust should apply to the federally regulated industries,[123] whether criminal sanctions should be repealed,[124] how much due process defendants and potential defendants should enjoy,[125] whether mergers should require advanced government notification or even approval,[126] and so forth.

But one conclusion seems inevitable: antitrust pervades a much wider area of American life, and involves much more fundamental issues, than is generally thought.

Nothing will ever make antitrust as exciting as sports, war or courtship. The primacy of such activities in exciting the human imagination must be acknowledged. But political issues without such combustible material have won popular attention in the past, and so may antitrust. If it does, two particular issues stand out which are most in need of popular resolution and are well adapted for it, since they involve political rather than economic judgments.

First, the basic question of the importance of efficiency must be settled. Are we as a people willing to give up greater production and a higher rate of growth for certain other objectives?

Second, and this issue is less readily expressed as a simple choice, do we as a people consider it desirable, if it is possible, to restore an earlier economic day of smaller firms, and, since the proportion has not in fact declined,[127] a higher proportion of independent businessmen?

After all, excitement and importance are not always the same thing. Luxuries are more exciting than necessities, but it is the necessities we need for existence. As Disraeli[128] once put the matter:

Man has deified corn and wine. But not even the Irish or the Chinese have erected temples to tea and potatoes.

Antitrust may be the tea and potatoes of our national economic policy. It is natural for man to run after more luxurious and esoteric goals. But our basic calories are still vital, and our basic policies still deserve a calmer and more rational popular and expert consideration than they are presently receiving.

NOTES

1. *U.S.* v. *Von's Grocery Co.*, 384 U.S. 270 (1966).
2. See Robert L. Bishop, "Monopolistic Competition and Welfare Econom-

ics," in Robert E. Keunne, ed., *Monopolistic Competition Theory: Studies in Impact* (New York: John Wiley & Sons, 1967), pp. 251-263.

3. *U.S. v. Von's Grocery Co.,* 384 U.S. 275 (1966).
4. See Daniel Hamberg, *R & D: Essays in the Economics of Research and Development* (New York: Random House, 1966), pp. 36-39.
5. *Ibid.,* pp. 45-68.
6. William Baumol, *Business Behavior, Value and Growth,* 2nd ed. (New York: Harcourt, Brace & World, 1967).
7. George J. Stigler, "Monopoly and Oligopoly by Merger," *American Economic Review Supplement,* XL (1950), 23ff.
8. *Standard Oil Co. v. U.S.,* 221 U.S. 1 (1911); *U.S. v. American Tobacco Co.,* 221 U.S. 106 (1911).
9. Stigler, "Monopoly and Oligopoly by Merger," p. 30.
10. See R. C. Dixon, "European Policies on Restrictive Business Practices," *American Economic Review Supplement,* XLVIII (1958), 442ff.
11. *U.S. v. Philadelphia Nat. Bank,* 374 U.S. 321, 365 note 42 (1963).
12. *U.S. v. Paramount Pictures,* 334 U.S. 131 (1948).
13. *Brown Shoe Co. v. U.S.,* 370 U.S. 294 (1962).
14. *U.S. v. Von's Grocery Co.,* 384 U.S. 270 (1966).
15. See F. D. Holzman, "Creeping Inflation," *Review of Economics and Statistics,* XLI (1959), 324ff.; J. D. Pitchford, "Cost and Demand Elements in the Inflationary Process," *Review of Economic Studies,* XXIV (1957), 139ff.
16. H. D. Henderson, "The Price System," *Economic Journal,* LVIII (1948), 467ff. An account of British price reactions to the outbreak of World War II in 1939.
17. Joseph A. Schumpeter, *The Theory of Economic Development* (New York: Oxford University Press, 1961); *Capitalism, Socialism and Democracy* (New York: Harper & Row, Publishers, 1962); *Business Cycles* (New York: McGraw-Hill Book Company, 1939). These are paperback editions.
18. John Kenneth Galbraith, *American Capitalism: The Concept of Countervailing Power* (Boston: Houghton, Mifflin Co., 1952).
19. Adolf A. Berle, *The Twentieth Century Capitalist Revolution* (New York: Harcourt, Brace & World, 1954).
20. See Robert Dorfman, *The Price System* (Englewood Cliffs, N.J.: Prentice-Hall, Inc., 1964), pp. 126-146.
21. See David Schwartzman, "The Burden of Monopoly," *Journal of Political Economy,* LXVIII (1960), 627ff.
22. *U.S. v. Von's Grocery Co.,* 384 U.S. 278 (1966).
23. Schumpeter, *Economic Development,* pp. 212-255.
24. See Abba P. Lerner, "Savings and Investment: Definitions, Assumptions, Objectives," *Quarterly Journal of Economics,* LIII (1939), 611ff.
25. John Maynard Keynes, "William Stanley Jevons," *Journal of the Royal Statistical Society,* IC (1936), 516, 529ff.
26. See Mark S. Massel, *Competition and Monopoly: Legal and Economic Issues* (Garden City, N.Y.: Doubleday & Co., 1964), pp. 175-189.
27. Bethuel Webster, "The Use of Economic Experts in Antitrust Litigation," *Record,* XVII (1962), 456ff.
28. Schumpeter, *Economic Development,* p. 62.
29. Lucile Sheppard Keyes, "Price Discrimination in Law and Economics," *Southern Economic Journal,* XXVII (1961), 320ff.

30. Edward S. Mason, "Monopoly in Law and Economics," *Yale Law Journal*, XLVII (1937), 34ff.
31. Richard C. Bernhard, "The Law and the Economics of Market Collusion in Europe, Great Britain, and the United States: An American Point of View," *Journal of Industrial Economics*, XIV (1966), 101, 116ff.
32. *FTC v. R. F. Keppel & Bros., Inc.*, 291 U.S. 304, 314 (1934).
33. *FTC v. Cement Inst.*, 333 U.S. 683 (1948).
34. U.S., *Const.*, Art. I, Sect. 8.
35. See G. E. Hale and R. D. Hale, "Mergers in Regulated Industries," *Northwestern University Law Review*, LIX (1964), 49ff.; "Symposium on Antitrust in the Regulated Industries," *Antitrust Bulletin*, XI (1966), 1ff.; *Northern Pacific Ry. Co. v. U.S.*, 356 U.S. 1 (1958).
36. *Apex Hosiery Co. v. Leader*, 310 U.S. 469 (1940).
37. Donald S. Watson, *Economic Policy: Business and Government* (Boston: Houghton, Mifflin Co., 1960), pp. 312-314, pp. 341-343.
38. See J. J. Hanson, "Comparison of State and Federal Antitrust Laws in Selected Areas," *A. B. A. Antitrust Section*, XXIX (1965), 267ff.
39. But see *U.S. v. Aluminum Co. of America*, 148 F. 2d 416 (2nd Cir., 1945), the sole Justice Department case appealed to a court of appeals, a widely criticized opinion.
40. *U.S. v. Singer Mfg. Co.*, 374 U.S. 174, 175 note 1 (1963).
41. Watson, *Economic Policy: Business and Government*, p. 267.
42. See Note: "Antitrust Significance of Covenants Not to Compete," *Michigan Law Review*, LXV (1966), 403ff.; *Summerhoys v. Scher*, 10 Cal. App. 574, 52 P. 2d 512 (1935); *Beit v. Beit*, 135 Conn. 195, 63 A. 2d 161 (1948).
43. See Richard E. Low, "The Failing Company Doctrine: An Illusive Economic Defense Under Section 7 of the Clayton Act," *Fordham Law Review*, XXXV (1967), 425ff.
44. *Standard Oil Co. v. U.S.*, 221 U.S. 60 (1911).
45. *Northern Pacific Ry. Co. v. U.S.*, 356 U.S. 5 (1958).
46. *Brown Shoe Co. v. U.S.*, 370 U.S. 346 (1962).
47. Jesse W. Markham, "Merger Policy Under the New Section 7: A Six-Year Appraisal," *Virginia Law Review*, XLIII (1957), 495ff.
48. House Report 1191, 81st. Cong., 1st. Sess., Committee on the Judiciary, 6 (1949).
49. See *Brown Shoe Co. v. U.S.*, 370 U.S. 11 (1962), note 13, Records and Briefs, "Brief for the Brown Shoe Company."
50. See Leo Loevinger, "The Rule of Reason in Antitrust Law," *Virginia Law Review*, L (1964), 23ff.
51. Carl Kaysen, *United States v. United Shoe Machinery Corporation: An Economic Analysis of an Antitrust Case* (Cambridge, Mass.: Harvard University Press, 1956), pp. 30-31.
52. *U.S. v. Pabst Brewing Co.*, 384 U.S. 546 (1966).
53. *Northern Pacific Ry. Co. v. U.S.*, 356 U.S. 5(1958), note 35.
54. See *U.S. v. Socony-Vacuum Oil Co.*, 310 U.S. 150 (1940); *Holophane Co. v. U.S.*, 352 U.S. 903 (1956); *Radovich v. Nat. Football League*, 352 U.S. 445 (1957); *Northern Pacific Ry. Co. v. U.S.*, 356 U.S. 5 (1958), note 35; *U.S. v. Loew's, Inc.*, 371 U.S. 38 (1962).
55. Milton Friedman, *Capitalism and Freedom* (Chicago: University of Chicago Press, 1962), pp. 129-131.

56. Lester Telser, "Abusive Trade Practices and Economic Analysis," *Law and Contemporary Problems,* XXX (1965), 488ff.

57. See Robert H. Bork and Ward S. Bowman, "Contrasts in Antitrust Theory," *Columbia Law Review,* LXV (1965), 3ff.

58. *Chicago Board of Trade* v. *U.S.,* 246 U.S. 231 (1918); *Appalachian Coals, Inc.* v. *U.S.,* 288 U.S. 344 (1933).

59. *U.S.* v. *Jerrold Electronics Corp.,* 187 F. Supp. 545, 571 (E.D. Pa. 1960).

60. *U.S.* v. *Aluminum Co. of America,* 377 U.S. 271, 279 (1964).

61. *Attorney-General's Committee, Report of the* (Washington: Government Printing Office, 1955), pp. 318ff.

62. Emanuel Celler, "Corporation Mergers and Antitrust Laws," *Mercer Law Review,* VII (1956), 269ff.

63. Compare national reports in "Symposium on Monopoly and Competition in Various Countries," in Edward H. Chamberlin, ed., *Monopoly and Competition and Their Regulation* (London: St. Martin's Press, 1954), pp. 3ff.

64. Carl Kaysen and Donald J. Turner, *Antitrust Policy: A Legal and Economic Analysis* (Cambridge, Mass.: Harvard University Press, 1959), pp. 98-99.

65. See Corwin D. Edwards, "Public Policy and Business Size," *The Journal of Business of the University of Chicago,* XXIV (1951), 280ff.

66. *FTC* v. *Consolidated Foods,* 380 U.S. 592 (1965), Records and Briefs, "Brief on Competition by the Consolidated Food Corporation."

67. See William Fellner, *Probability and Profit* (Homewood, Ill.: Richard D. Irwin, Inc., 1965).

68. Adam Smith, *The Wealth of Nations* (London: Cannan Ed., 1930), I, 130ff.

69. See Joe S. Bain, *Barriers to New Competition* (Cambridge, Mass.: Harvard University Press, 1956).

70. *Brown Shoe Co.* v. *U.S.,* 370 U.S. 320 (1962), note 13.

71. *U.S.* v *Von's Grocery Co.,* 384 U.S. 281 (1966), note 1.

72. *Ibid.,* 275.

73. *Ibid.,* 273, 277.

74. See Joe S. Bain, "Economies of Scale, Concentration, and the Condition of Entry in Twenty Manufacturing Industries," *American Economic Review,* XLIV (1954), 15ff.

75. See *A. G. Spalding & Bros., Inc.* v. *FTC,* 301 F. 2d 585 (3rd Cir. 1962), Records and Briefs, "Brief for the Federal Trade Commission," 57 "Brief for the A. G. Spalding & Bros., Inc. Company," 52-53.

76. *Brown Shoe Co.* v. *U.S.,* 370 U.S. 322 (1962), note 13.

77. *U.S.* v. *Von's Grocery Co.,* 384 U.S. 280, 281 (1962), note 1.

78. See *American Crystal Sugar Co.* v. *Cuban American Sugar Co.,* 259 F. 2d 528 (2nd Cir. 1958), Records and Briefs, "Reply Brief of the Cuban American Sugar Company," 2-4.

79. *Crown Zellerbach Corp.* v. *FTC,* 156 F. 2d 927 (9th Cir. 1961), Records and Briefs, "Reply Brief for the Crown Zellerbach Corporation," 67.

80. *U.S.* v. *U.S. Steel Corp.,* 251 U.S. 417 (1920).

81. *U.S.* v. *Bethlehem Steel Corp.,* 168 F. Supp. 576 (S.D.N.Y., 1958); *U.S.* v. *Bliss & Laughlin, Inc.,* 302 F. Supp. 334 (S.D. Calif., 1962).

82. George J. Stigler, "The Kinky Oligopoly Demand Curve and Rigid Prices," *The Journal of Political Economy,* LV (1947), 432ff.

83. See B. M. Cheek, "Economic Theory and Industrial Pricing," *Economic Record Supplement,* XXV (1949), 140ff.

84. Stigler, "The Kinky Oligopoly Demand Curve and Rigid Prices," pp. 421-431.
85. *Scott Paper Co.* v. *FTC*, 301 F. 2d 579 (3rd Cir., 1962), Records and Briefs, "Briefs for the Scott Paper Company," 214a, 216a, "Proposed Findings of Fact and Conclusions of Law, for the Scott Paper Company," 167a.
86. Edward S. Mason, "Price and Production Policies of Large-Scale Enterprise," *American Economic Review Supplement,* XXIX (1939), 61, 65, note 9.
87. *FTC* v. *Consolidated Foods,* 380 U.S. 592 (1965), Records and Briefs, "Respondent's Exhibit 268," 2570.
88. *Scott Paper Co.* v. *FTC*, 301 F. 2d 579 (3rd Cir., 1962), Records and Briefs, "Proceedings Before the Hearing Examiner," 734a, 991a.
89. *U.S.* v. *Lever Bros. Co.,* 216 F. Supp. 887, 898 (S.D.N.Y., 1963).
90. Robert F. Lanzillotti, "The Automobile Industry," in Walter Adams, ed., *The Structure of American Industry,* 3rd ed. (New York: The Macmillan Company, 1961), pp. 336ff.
91. *Ibid.,* Walter Adams, "The Steel Industry," pp. 171-176.
92. *U.S.* v. *Aluminum Co. of America,* 148 F. 2d 431 (2nd Cir., 1945).
93. *U.S.* v. *Bethlehem Steel Corp.,* 168 F. Supp. 588 (S.D.N.Y., 1958).
94. John Maurice Clark, "Toward a Concept of Workable Competition," *American Economic Review,* XXX (1940), 241ff.; *Competition As a Dynamic Process* (Washington: Brookings Institution, 1961).
95. *Attorney-General's Comm.* (Washington: G.P.O., 1955), pp. 325-333.
96. *Brown Shoe Co.* v. *U.S.,* 370 U.S. 324 (1962).
97. Lanzillotti, "The Automobile Industry," pp. 332-333.
98. *U.S.* v. *Von's Grocery Co.,* 384 U.S. 277 (1966).
99. *Brown Shoe Co.* v. *U.S.,* 370 U.S. 322 (1962).
100. *Scott Paper Co.* v. *FTC*, 301 F. 2d 582 (3rd Cir., 1962).
101. *U.S.* v. *Aluminum Co. of America,* 377 U.S. 273ff. (1964).
102. *Scott Paper Co.* v. *FTC*, 301 F. 2d 583 (3rd Cir., 1962).
103. *A. G. Spalding & Bros., Inc.* v. *FTC*, 301 F. 2d 595 (3rd Cir., 1962).
104. *U.S.* v. *Aluminum Co. of America,* 148 F. 2d 432 (2nd Cir., 1945).
105. *A. G. Spalding & Bros., Inc.* v. *FTC*, 301 F. 2d 584 (3rd Cir., 1962).
106. Matthew Josephson, *The Robber Barons* (New York: Harcourt, Brace & World, 1934), pp. 375-403.
107. *Standard Oil Co.* v. *U.S.,* 221 U.S. 1 (1911).
108. *U.S.* v. *Von's Grocery Co.,* 384 U.S. 270 (1966); *Brown Shoe Co.* v. *U.S.,* 370 U.S. 294 (1962).
109. *U.S.* v. *U.S. Steel Corp.,* 251 U.S. 417 (1920).
110. Edward S. Mason, "The Current Status of the Monopoly Problem in the United States," *Harvard Law Review,* LXII (1949), 1265, 1273.
111. Walter Adams, "The Steel Industry," pp. 171ff.
112. *U.S.* v. *Bethlehem Steel Corp.,* 168 F. Supp. 576 (S.D.N.Y., 1958).
113. *U.S.* v. *Von's Grocery Co.,* 384 U.S. 272 (1966); *Brown Shoe Co.* v. *U.S.,* 370 U.S. 294ff. (1962).
114. *U.S.* v. *Von's Grocery Co.,* 384 U.S. 281ff (1966).
115. See Dorfman, *The Price System,* pp. 126-145.
116. Harvey Leibenstein, "Allocative Efficiency v. 'X-Efficiency,'" *American Economic Review,* LXI (1966), 392ff.
117. Edward H. Chamberlin, *The Theory of Monopolistic Competition,* 8th ed. Cambridge, Mass.: Harvard University Press, 1962), pp. 110ff.

118. *Cf. U.S.* v. *Kennecott Copper Corp.*, 231 F. Supp. 95, 103 (S.D.N.Y., 1964) War on Communism is held an antimerger factor.
119. *Attorney-General's Committee, Report of the*, pp. 5-8.
120. *U.S.* v. *Von's Grocery Co.*, 384 U.S. 281ff. (1966).
121. See *U.S.* v. *Philadelphia Nat. Bank*, 374 U.S. 365 (1963).
122. See Tibor Scitovsky, *Welfare and Competition* (Chicago: Richard D. Irwin, Inc., 1951), pp. 323ff.
123. *Northern Pacific Ry. Co.* v. *U.S.*, 356 U.S. 1 (1958); *Pan American World Airways, Inc.* v. *U.S.*, 371 U.S. 296 (1963).
124. Kaysen and Turner, *Antitrust Policy*, p. 91.
125. Philip Elman, "The Federal Trade Commission and the Administrative Process," *Antitrust Bulletin*, VIII (1963), 607ff.
126. Celler, "Corporation Mergers and Antitrust Laws."
127. Jesse W. Markham, "The New Antitrust Policy and the Individual Business Firm," *Law and Contemporary Problems*, XXX (1965), pp. 607ff. (From a section not included in the reprint here.)
128. Benjamin Disraeli, *Coningsby or The New Generation* (New York: New American Library, 1962), p. 135.

PART I

How Competitive Is the American Economy?

MONOPOLY AND CONCENTRATION: COMPARISONS IN TIME AND SPACE

Morris A. Adelman

Morris A. Adelman is Professor of Economics at the Massachusetts Institute of Technology. He is the author of A&P: Study in Price-Cost Behavior and Public Policy (Cambridge, Mass.: Harvard University Press, 1959) and has served as an antitrust economic consultant for the du Pont Corporation and for other defendants.

A celebrated author of our time has said: "All my life, I have had a certain idea of France, as much from sentiment as from logic." If General de Gaulle permitted me, I would say that most economists and non-economists, throughout their lives, have had a certain idea of monopoly, produced more by sentiment, or at least habit, than by analysis. The predominant idea of monopoly in the literature, best seen when mentioned incidentally, exposing basic notions in an obliquely revealing light, like late afternoon sunshine, is basically that of *size*. Monopoly means big business, modern industry, thousands of employees, multi-millions and billions in assets, worldwide operations, etc. . . .

The idea of monopoly increasing inevitably along with the development of industry probably originated with Karl Marx, who in a well known passage prophesied that ownership of capital goods would become ever more concentrated into fewer hands, until at

This article first appeared in the form of testimony before the Senate Antitrust and Monopoly subcommittee. Reprinted by permission of the University of Padua.

last the Revolution would come and "the expropriators are expropriated." The theoretical foundation, never explicitly stated, seems to have been a belief in ever-increasing economies of scale. Whatever the reason, the idea of increasing concentration and monopoly took firm hold of both the profession and of lay opinion, so that as late as 1941 one reads in an excellent Cambridge economic handbook that "the nineteenth century . . . was a century of competition, the twentieth one of monopoly." Since then, the accumulation of data has destroyed this generalization, until now the question is whether one ought not to do with Marx what he said he did with Hegel—turn him upside down in order to set him right side up, and say that the degree of monopoly lessens as industry develops. . . . His basic error was simple and very close to another one he made: that the ratio of capital to labor was on the increase because of greater mechanization. Since profit, in the Marxist view, derived only from labor, the rate of profit had to be fatally on the decrease. The process could indeed be slowed by what Marx, always an excellent observer, called "cheapening of capital." But the fall in its price might be less or more or about the same as, the growth—in some sense or other—of its physical mass. The capital-labor ratio, or "organic composition," can therefore rise or fall, and has not continually increased.

Similarly, if industrial progress means increasing economies of scale, the occasion and necessary condition for them is the increase of the market. . . . Economies of scale may increase faster *or* slower than the market, and there is no general or a priori reason to suppose that the number of viable firms in any given market must increase or decrease. Hence there is no reason to expect greater concentration, on the average, in the markets composing the economy. . . .

No general theory has yet been propounded which seems inherently more convincing than any other. In this essay we first maintain that the concentration ratio which has become familiar in the United States is so far the closest approximation to monopoly in the sense of economic theory; we distinguish between concentration in industries or markets on the one side, and broad aggregations such as the largest hundred or five hundred firms in the whole economy, or all manufacturing, etc.; we then look at development of both kinds of concentration in the United States over approximately the past half century, try some comparisons among various countries, and finally indicate what general observations may legitimately be made.

THE MEANING OF CONCENTRATION

The size of a business firm may be measured by its assets, employees, income generated, etc. "Absolute size is absolutely irrelevant to market control." The simple fact of size is often hidden by calling it "economic power," or adding even more confusion with "countervailing power," etc., phrases which mix up two altogether different concepts. One is economies of scale: the "power" to attain lower costs, and within what limits. The other "power" is control of supply (or of demand)—the ability to affect the price by putting more or less of one's product or service onto the market.

Statistics of concentration attempt to measure indirectly what cannot be seen directly—few or many firms in any given market. . . . The fewer the firms, everything else being equal, the easier it is to collaborate and so align price and production policies as at least to travel a goodly way, or nearly all the way, toward monopoly.

Fewness is not necessarily non-competitive in any given instance. Easy substitution of factors or products may mean that even complete occupancy of the industry gives no power over price. Many circumstances may force the few to act willy-nilly in complete independence, not merely in the American legal sense of non-communication with rivals, but in the economic sense of each firm always seeking its own profit, neither trying to serve the group interest, nor expecting anyone else to do so. The key condition is mutual independence, for which large numbers are not necessary but usually suffice. . . .

Although few or many firms are what we are trying to measure, we can not simply count the number of firms in any industry or market. The number of firms is often not only difficult but probably impossible to determine. The boundaries of an industry cannot be precisely laid down, and it is at the boundaries that one finds a large number of small operators. The distinction between a firm and a self-employed individual is often vague. The number of firms may vary from season to season. Their product mix may be such as to make comparisons among them of doubtful meaning, even if they must for purposes of classifications be put in one or another statistical box. Indeed, the U.S. Census Bureau must arbitrarily throw large numbers of firms into one or another industry in "job lots" because they must be put some place; they are so small that it does not make any difference for the totals of value added, sales, employment, etc., where they are put, and it would be a prohibitive expense to count them accurately.

But even if we could count the number of firms in any given industry, we would still not have a useful number for measuring fewness or many-ness because of the great inequality of firm size. Where, for example, one firm had 95 per cent of a market and 100 other firms, all very small, occupied the other 5 per cent, it would be formally true to say that there were 101 firms in the industry, but for understanding the workings of the industry, we would be much nearer the truth in calling this a one-firm industry than a 101-firm industry. Hence, inequality destroys any hope of a simple count of firms.

Inequality does not mean anything more than this. . . . Success and survival depend on costs, prices, and all else that makes a market. Mere inequality of size has nothing to do with "bargaining power," which is just another name for the degree of monopoly. To know that a firm is a certain per cent of a market is at least the first step in describing that market. That one firm is many times as large as another implies nothing. . . .

Concentration deals, therefore, with *numbers modified by inequality:* an approximate answer to the question of whether a given industry consists of few or many firms.

As indicated earlier, if substitutes are close, entry easy, etc., the boundaries of the market mean little, and few-ness is more apparent than real. There is no strong connection between concentration and any behavior pattern in any instance. But, as a general statistical matter, the greater the concentration the lower the odds in favor of competitive behavior. Therefore, though a single concentration ratio tells us little about a given industry at a given time, comparisons over time or among countries, or regions, or industries at the same time, do convey information; a concentration ratio might be regarded as an index number, meaningless in itself, indispensable for comparison—*provided* the biases have approximately the same mean and variance, and we must admit there is little evidence on this one way or another.

The concentration ratio, the holding of the largest n firms (four in the U.S.), is a crude approximation, but so far it is the only thing we have which fits the requirements of economic theory that it have some relevance to market behavior. . . .

INDUSTRY AND PRODUCT CONCENTRATION, 1901-1958

Table 1 presents a summary view of concentration in the U.S. over the past sixty-odd years. The technique is simple. For each comparison, e.g., between 1901 and 1947, or between 1954 and 1958, the industries are classed in the same groups, or as near to it as the data will permit. For each industry designated by a four-digit number, we compute the "concentration ratio," i.e., the percentage of sales accounted for by the four largest firms. The weighting factor of each industry is its value added (the difference between its purchases and its sales) which measures its own contribution to the national product. For 1901, where the figures are more rough, we must make do with using the value added by the individual four-digit industries with a concentration ratio over 50 as a per cent of value added by all industries in the large two-digit industry group. But for later years we are able to use a more precise measure. If we multiply each industry's concentration ratio by its weighting factor, then add up all the resulting numbers and divide by the total value-added, we have a *weighted average concentration ratio*. Table 1 shows the weighted average concentration ratio for the twenty industry groups, each designated by a two-digit number, and in the bottom line shows the weighted average for all Census industries.

The measure appears to have declined substantially from 1901 to 1947, and not to have changed much since then. I say "appears to have" advisedly: we must be cautious in interpreting data as imperfect as those we have for the early period. To be sure, they were published estimates, subject to informed criticism by people who knew enough of the industries to question a radically wrong estimate, and suggest a better. Hence they cannot be called wide of

TABLE 1

Average concentration ratios value added by 4-digit industries with over 50 concentration ratios as a % of value added by all industries in a 2-digit group[1]

Industry[2]	1901[3]	1947[4]	1947[4]	1954[5]	1958[6]
			Average Concentration		
20 Food and kindred products	39.1	18.8	34.9	33.8	32.6
21 Tobacco manufactures	49.9	77.7	76.2	73.4	74.1
22 Textile mill products	20.3	9.0	24.3	26.5	29.2
23 Apparel and related products	—	2.2	12.6	13.0	13.4
24 Lumber and wood products	0.5	2.0	11.2	10.8	12.8
25 Furniture and fixtures	—	8.1	21.9	20.3	19.0
26 Pulp, paper, and products	71.0	1.6	21.2	24.8	25.9
27 Printing and publishing	1.0	0.0	19.7	17.7	17.6
28 Chemicals and related products	24.3	33.7	51.0	48.6	45.7
29 Petroleum and coal products	46.8	13.6	39.5	36.6	31.6[9]
30 Rubber products	100.0	59.9	58.6	54.1	51.3
31 Leather and leather products	26.3	0.0	26.2	26.4	25.0
32 Stone, clay, and glass products	13.3	43.9	43.4	46.4	40.3[10]
33 Primary metal products	45.7[7]	21.0	43.8	49.5	46.8
34 Fabricated metal products	—	8.4	25.3	26.1	25.5
35 Machinery, except electrical	41.4[8]	18.5	38.0	33.2	35.5
36 Electrical machinery	—	53.2	54.1	48.2	46.9
37 Transportation equipment	57.3	84.2	54.4	58.7	61.3
38 Instruments and related products	—	45.0	45.3	47.4	47.8
39 Miscellaneous manufactures	2.7	21.2	34.9	16.1	22.6
Total, all industries	32.9	24.0	35.3	36.9	37.0

[1] In the absence of complete data for 1901, this measure was substituted for average concentration with value-added weights. The correspondence between these two measures depends upon the extent to which the frequency distribution of 4-digit concentration ratios, with value added measuring frequency, retained the same general shape in 1947 as in 1901.

[2] 1947 and 1954 Census Classification.

[3] 319 (4-digit) industries. Various years 1895-1904; central date was approximately 1901 but weighting used was as of 1899.

[4] 452 (4-digit) industries.

[5] 434 (4-digit) industries.

[6] 439 (4-digit) industries.

[7] Excludes steel works and rolling mills for which concentration was 78.8%.

[8] Includes electrical machinery.

[9] In this year industry 2931, Beehive Coke Ovens, and industry 2932, Byproduct

the mark. But the limits of possible error are wide enough to include the apparent decrease. The only safe conclusion, I believe, is that there was at least no increase. Since 1947, it is apparent that there has been a considerable change in many four-digit industries, but the ups have about offset the downs.

So much for the weighted average measure. There is also sense in looking not at averages but rather frequency distributions. For concentration could be stable, on the average, either because most industries were stable, or because in most industries concentration was really increasing, but in a few large ones was decreasing. Table 2 therefore presents a frequency distribution by industries, and it is apparent that so far as number of industries is concerned, there seem to have been, during the post-war, about as many decreases as increases.

The 450-odd industries produced just over 1,000 products. Comparison of product concentration can be made in two ways, each of them instructive. First, as in Table 3, which is confined to only 472 of the approximate 1,000 products, because only for that number are the figures comparable as between 1954 and 1958. The increases of 10 or more per cent points are about equal to the decreases; there were somewhat more decreases of between 5 and 9 points than increases; about 61 per cent of all products stayed in the range between −4 and +4 per cent—effectively zero change. This group of 472 products is a biased collection, precisely because the product classes are comparable; they ignore that majority of products which have changed.

Table 4 compares the distribution of product groups without regard to comparability. Thus we are unable to speak of increases or decreases of concentration in any given product, but simply to

---

Coke Ovens, were lumped together into industry 3312, Blast Furnaces and Steel Mills.

[10] Industry 3273, Ready-Mixed Concrete, was included for the first time in 1958.

Sources:

1. U. S. Bureau of the Census, *Historical Statistics of the United States, Colonial Times to 1957*, Washington, D. C., 1960, p. 573.
2. U. S. Bureau of the Census, *U. S. Census of Manufactures*, 1958, Vol. 1, Summary Statistics, Washington, D. C., 1961, Appendix C.
3. U. S. Bureau of the Census, *Concentration Ratios in Manufacturing Industry*, 1958, Washington, D. C., 1962, Table 2.

TABLE 2

Distribution of industries (4-digit) based on percentage point changes in value of shipments, 4-firm concentration ratios between 1947 and 1958

Change	Number	% of Industries
Increase		
10 or more points	39	8.7
5 to 9 points	55	12.3
Increase of 4 points to		
decrease of 4 points	168	37.7
Decrease		
5 to 9 points	54	12.1
10 or more points	44	9.9
Not available[1]	86	19.3
Totals	446	100.0

[1] The not available group includes those ratios which were unobtainable, withheld to prevent disclosure, or noncomparable within the period.

Source: U. S. Bureau of the Census, *Concentration Ratios in Manufacturing Industry*, 1958 (Washington, 1962), Table 2, pp. 10–42.

compare the grouping of products by concentration ratios in the earlier and later years. As the table shows, there was apparently a shift toward more classes with lower concentration.

TABLE 3

Distribution of product classes (5-digit) by percentage point change in 4-firm, value of shipments concentration ratios for 1954–58
(comparable product classes only)

Change	Number	Per Cent of Product Classes
Increase		
10 or more points	21	4.4
5 to 9 points	59	12.5
Increase of 4 points to		
decrease of 4 points	290	61.4
Decrease		
5 to 9 points	81	17.2
10 or more points	21	4.4
Totals[1]	472	100.0

[1] Figures may not add to sum due to rounding.

Source: U. S. Bureau of the Census, *Concentration Ratios in Manufacturing Industry*, 1958 (Washington, 1962), Table 4, pp. 107-165.

Now, if we ask whether Table 1 and Tables 3 and 4 are reconcilable or not, we are forced to recognize a difference between industries and products. An industry is a collection of plants, each of which may turn out more than one product. There is some force in the idea that, since competition is essentially concerned with products, the product results are really much more relevant for our purposes than the industry results, and therefore that the picture of slowly diminishing concentation among products should blot out the picture of no change among industries. I cannot agree; a firm is an assemblage of facilities, and of people with know-how, who can turn out one or another product mix as seems most advantageous to them. For understanding markets, the capacity represented by a plant is at least as important as the temporary embodiment of that capacity in one or another product mix in any short period. Moreover, industries can be given weights, and then added up. We cannot do this with

TABLE 4

Distribution of product classes (5-digit) by concentration ratio for 4 firms, based on value of shipments: 1954-1958

Concentration	1954		1958	
Class	Number	Per Cent	Number	Per Cent
0-9	28	2.7	32	3.0
10-19	119	11.6	112	10.6
20-29	151	14.7	178	16.9
30-39	159	15.5	166	15.8
40-49	154	15.0	155	14.7
50-59	124	12.1	126	12.0
60-69	101	9.9	82	7.8
70-79	72	7.0	69	6.6
80-89	52	5.1	44	4.2
90-100	37	3.6	35	3.3
Not Available[1]	28	2.7	54	5.1
Totals[2]	1,025	100.0	1,053	100.0

[1] The not available group includes those ratios which were unobtainable, withheld to prevent disclosure, and noncomparable with product classes bearing the same title in earlier years. In 1958 there were 164, and in 1954, 99 product classes for product divisions "not specified by kind," and these were omitted from all tabulations and totals because a concentration ratio is impossible to compute for these classes.

[2] Figures may not add to sum due to rounding.

Sources: Concentration in American Industry (Washington, 1957), Table 37. *Concentration Ratios in Manufacturing Industry*, 1958, Table 4.

products, because we cannot usually allocate the value added of the establishment to individual products.

I think we gain more enlightenment by looking at both measures than by choosing one or the other. If weighted average industry concentration seems to have remained stable, while product concentration has decreased, this suggests a single hypothesis which will reconcile both of these facts—namely, that firms have tended to diversify within their respective broad industry grouping. Thus the comparison of two separate measures gives us an additional bit of information about industry structure.

"OVER-ALL CONCENTRATION"

I turn now to a very different subject, "concentration" not in individual industries or industry groups, but in very broad classifications such as all non-financial corporations, or all manufacturing, etc. It is unfortunate that the same term "concentration" should be applied to statistics of this kind, for there is no logical relation between the two kinds of measurements.

It is logical to aggregate the largest firms in a given market, for in theory, the fewer the firms and the more they hold, all being equal, the nearer to monopoly. There is no such rationale in the aggregating of several dozen or hundred firms into such broad groups as manufactures, public utilities, etc. There may be some other perfectly good reasons for making aggregations of this kind. . . . But we can say nothing about market structure, market behavior, competition, prices, production, etc., after viewing statistics of "over-all concentration."

Moreover, a little reflection will show that concentration could be increasing in every single industry, and the more concentrated industries could even be growing more quickly than the less concentrated industries, yet "over-all concentration" could be decreasing and vice versa. Aggregating corporations this way across industries mixes up changes in concentration with variations in growth rates of big-firm industries and small-firm industries, and the size of an industry and of its firms does not correlate with concentration. . . .

In the past, use has sometimes been made of the 200 largest non-financial corporations, including public utilities. There would be little doubt that concentration increased in the late 1920's, specifically from 1924 to 1929, and has declined since, owing to the Public Utilities Holding Companies Act. (Over half the 1929 assets of this group were public utilities.) But if we are primarily interested in the operation of economic forces, as distinct from the contribution of government, I think it well to lay utilities aside, and this reduces us largely to manufacturing. Non-manufacturing is important, but we cannot get the necessary comparable figures.

Looking then at manufacturing, we have got to face the absence of any reasonably good and comparable set of corporate reports before 1931. Take one obvious point: treating accumulated depreciation as an addition to liabilities rather than a subtraction from assets can make capital assets twice as big as if depreciation were subtracted from assets. Moreover, as Edwin B. George once put it, any such comparisons become arguments about which capitalization figures had how much more fiction in them, and "tend to throw us away from a measurement of finite bodies and toward one that could well bear the title, 'A Few Speculative Thoughts on the Effect of Assumed Leverages on Unknown Weights.'"

Our data really begins in 1931, when the Internal Revenue Service began publishing corporate balance sheets by asset size classes and industry groups. These we have for every year except 1934-41, which are not comparable because of a change in the tax laws. These figures are all entered subject to the same set of accounting definitions, and, of course, with some substantial penalties for false statements. For corporate financial statistics, prehistory ends in 1931, and history begins.

Table 5 shows the share of assets held by the largest firms in manufacturing for every available year since 1931. The number of companies in the largest size class increases because of economic growth and often price increases. Twice the lower limit of the largest size class was increased, from 50 to 100 million, then to 250 million dollars, diminishing the number in the topmost class. We must look carefully for years which have almost the same number of largest firms and then a small adjustment can be made safely, to add the proper number of firms and credit them with the minimum value for the class just above it. Table 6 shows the share of the largest 117 firms from 1931 to the present, but omits all the years for which we either have no data or for which the number of firms

TABLE 5

Largest manufacturing firms

Year	Largest Asset Class ($ 1,000)	Number of Largest Firms	Total Assets ($ 1,000)	Largest Firms' Assets ($ 1,000)	Largest Firms' Share of Assets (%)
1931	50,000	139	63,802	29,646	46.5
1932	50,000	117	59,023	27,295	46.2
1933	50,000	119	57,753	26,436	45.8
1942	100,000	112	85,092	35,285	41.5
1943	100,000	127	94,767	41,597	43.9
1944	100,000	126	95,999	41,774	43.5
1945	100,000	120	91,030	38,470	42.3
1946	100,000	116	96,300	37,310	38.7
1947	100,000	133	111,355	45,082	40.5
1948	100,000	144	121,708	51,458	42.3
1949	100,000	144	123,755	53,628	43.3
1950	100,000	170	141,600	63,073	44.5
1951	100,000	199	160,876	75,700	47.1
1952	100,000	215	170,282	84,031	49.3
1953	100,000	223	176,805	90,024	50.9
1954	250,000	91	181,891	74,437	40.9
1955	250,000	97	201,360	84,246	41.8
1956	250,000	101	216,363	91,406	42.2
1957	250,000	107	224,910	99,634	44.3
1958	250,000	114	235,836	104,808	44.4
1959	250,000	121	252,134	113,202	44.9
1960	250,000	125	262,308	118,993	45.4
1961	250,000	134	275,964	129,042	46.8

Source: Internal Revenue Service, *Statistics of Income; Corporation Returns.*

are so different that we cannot safely compare them. We use the number of 117 firms merely because that permits us to make the most comparisons with the least adjustments, but if we also were to try 107 firms, 119 firms, or 133 firms, the picture would not change. There was an increase from 1931 to 1932 and then a decrease; an increase from 1942 to 1943, a decrease through 1946, a decrease from 1957 through 1959, and then a slight increase to 1960.

There is room for at least three hypotheses: first, as suggested by Willard F. Mueller, a cyclical movement. But this implies a regular recurrent motion, for which in my opinion there is too little evidence. The second hypothesis is: an irregular fluctuation. The

TABLE 6

Assets for the equivalent of 117 firms

Year	Number of Firms in Highest Size Class[1]	Unadjusted Share of Total Assets	Required Adjustment	Adjusted Share (117 firms)
1931	139	46.5	Subtract 22	44.7
1932	117	46.2	None	46.2
1933	119	45.8	Subtract 2	45.6
1942	112	41.5	Add 5	42.0
1943	127	43.9	Subtract 10	42.8
1944	126	43.5	Subtract 9	42.6
1945	120	42.3	Subtract 3	41.9
1946	116	38.7	Add 1	38.8
1947		omit		
1948		"		
1949		"		
1950		"		
1951		"		
1952		"		
1953		"		
1954		"		
1955		"		
1956		"		
1957	107	44.3	Add 10	45.4
1958	114	44.4	Add 3	44.8
1959	121	44.9	Subtract 4	44.5
1960	125	45.4	Subtract 8	44.6

[1] In 1931-37, $ 50 millions; 1942-53, $ 100 millions; thereafter $ 250 millions.

third would be: no real change in the underlying data, but the disturbances of depression, war, and reconstruction generating some meaningless change in the observations. My own feeling is that the truth lies somewhere between the second and third hypotheses, but there is no way of rigorously disproving either. Perhaps later research will tell us more.

One hypothesis cannot be reconciled with these data: any long-term increase in "over-all concentration."

There are some technical problems involved here. In particular, there was undoubtedly less consolidation of assets in the early 1930's, thereby understating concentration and hiding a downtrend. This was not necessarily serious, unless some of the affiliates or subsidiaries of the largest companies were also counted among the largest companies; we cannot tell. Two pieces of independent evidence indicate that consolidation is no problem in the late 1950's and 1960's. First, assets as measured by the IRS are almost the same as assets measured by the Quarterly Financial Report series, which are completely consolidated.

Second, if we compare receipts of manufacturing corporations as computed by the Census Bureau and the Internal Revenue Service, the difference is less than two-thirds of one per cent.

The chances are that there was some understatement of concentration in the early 1930's, and hence that the real change should have been somewhat more negative than we have here. I doubt that this is of any substantial importance: over a long time period, the effect of errors in the levels in the terminal years is small. Since we do now have a long time, it is unlikely that technical adjustments would have much effect on the comparison.

I see no possible escape from the conclusion that "over-all concentration" in the largest manufacturing firms has remained quite stable over a period of 30 years, from 1931 to 1961. I cannot conceive of any circumstances which could so effect the statistics that they failed to register an increasing concentration, taking place over so long a period of time.

There is another set of figures which cover part of this ground, but they are even more skimpy. For 1937, the 50 manufacturing companies, largest in sales, accounted for 20.2 per cent of value added by manufacture. This must be an underestimate, since had we chosen the 50 largest by value added, there would have been a different 50, with a somewhat larger value added. We cannot tell by how much this understated the share in value added of the 50 largest firms—but certainly not more than 2 or 3 percentage points. The best we can say for 1937 is that the share of the largest 50 was somewhere between 20 and 23 per cent. In 1947, the corresponding figure was only 17 per cent, in 1954 and again in 1958 it was 23 per cent. It is, therefore, hard to argue with the conclusion that this percentage has not changed much in recent years. As with our other figures, there is room for differences of opinion over whether we have a cycle or irregular fluctuations, or anything else, and of course, we are even worse off with these figures than with the asset figures, because we have only three observations over a period of 21 years.

Given these few data, it is curious how ready some men have been to draw the most complex and sweeping conclusions from them. For example, the idea of drastically increasing diversification of the large companies, who were not increasing their share of any of the particular industries, but were branching into other industries. This was a logical possibility, but possibility is not probability, let alone established fact. In any case, Nelson's study shows that the reason for the 1947-1954 increase was, first the drastic growth in the size of aircraft companies after the outbreak of the Korean War; second, an increase in concentration in the automobile industry. The idea of increasing diversification leading to the change in the share of the largest fifty was examined and specifically rejected. To the same effect is such little evidence as we have on vertical integration. If there had been any substantial change in it, the volume of corporate sales would not have increased as fast as the growth in corporate output, and hence the ratio of income originating in corporate enterprise to corporate sales should have increased. This ratio has if anything tended to decrease since the end of World War II.

For manufacturing, it is possible to compare total corporate sales with total value-added, and again no tendency is discernible. It would be possible for a diversification movement to be going on without any effect on vertical integration, but it does not seem likely.

In any case, looking at this by figures, it is absolutely impossible to reconcile this with any thesis at all of increasing "over-all concentration."

We come now to the question of what mergers have contributed to the position of these largest 117-odd companies. For over a decade at least, year in and year out, we have had a flood of statements about the rising tide of mergers concentrating the economy, the grand sweep of twentieth-century events, etc. In 1955, a Federal Trade Commission publication got some way toward actual ascertainment and measurement; starting with their data, a rather crude estimate was that about two per cent of all manufacturing-mining corporate assets were involved in mergers during the years 1951-54. This was apparently too high. Again, thanks to Dr. Mueller, we have some estimates of the amount of assets involved in mergers from 1948 through 1963. Over the years 1948-1963, the amount of assets acquired by the largest companies amounted to approximately one-half of one per cent of total assets in any year of the largest. That is to say, since the largest 150-odd corporations, speaking now in round numbers, accounted for little short of 50 per cent of all manufacturing corporate assets, if they continued acquisitions at the same pace for 100 years, they would have swallowed up the other 50 per cent of the corporate universe—on condition that the rest of the universe kept quiet in the meantime, and refrained from growing. But since the economy does retain this habit, no prediction is justified.

Of the total growth of the assets of the largest companies, something like 16 per cent was due to acquisitions, and the other 84 due to internal growth. It does not follow that if these largest companies had not made any mergers, their assets today would be 16 per cent less than they actually are. First, an acquisition for cash or equivalent would not increase the assets of the acquiring firm at all. Since acquisitions averaged so small a per cent of the assets of the acquiring companies this imposed no strain on liquidity. Of course, it would be mistaken to take the average for all companies, one-half of one per cent, and suppose that each individual acquiring company paid that percentage of its assets; the actual percentage must have been considerably larger. But counterbalancing this to some extent is the fact that a given acquisition could be financed by cash accumulated over a period of more than one year.

The second reason why we cannot suppose that mergers were responsible for 16 per cent of the asset increase is that the acquisition of a going concern is only one method of acquiring additional facilities. The alternative is always to build rather than to buy. Had there been no convenient merger candidate available, the acquiring company would in most cases have raised and spent money for the new assets rather than a going concern. Indeed, since the bulk of mergers continued to be in the same broad industry class as the acquiring company, where it is most obviously possible to build instead of buying, it is a reasonable inference that the greater part of all mergers represents a growth that would have come about anyway. Therefore, it is probably stretching matters to suppose that as much as eight per cent of the growth of the very largest firms was due to mergers.

This may all be good or bad, but acquisitions have simply not had any kind of perceptible effect on "over-all concentration," which in turn has no logical connection at all with industrial concentration. And yet it might be embarrassing to cite the solemn disquisitions on why mergers were changing the structure of industries.

CONCLUSION

Concentration is high in many American industries, while "over-all concentration" is high in the manufacturing and public utility area. There is no sign at all of any abiding tendency to increase down to 1958 for the one and 1960 for the other. But it does not follow that because there was a zero trend up to 1958 or 1960 it continued in the years since. However frequent is extrapolation it is not for that reason any more respectable. . . .

THE ECONOMIC THEORY OF ANTITRUST:
SCIENCE OR RELIGION?

Donald Dewey

Donald Dewey is Professor of Economics at Columbia University. He is the author of Monopoly in Economics and Law (*Chicago: Rand, McNally & Co., 1959*).

INTRODUCTION

The late Henry Simons once complained that anyone who questions the merits of labor unions immediately places himself in the category of people who sneer at religion, monogamy, motherhood, or the home. It is also possible to enter this subversive company by questioning the aims and effects of the federal antitrust laws. In 1890 the Sherman Act was passed in haste and received with some suspicion and much indifference by lawyers and economists. Seventy-four years later the Sherman Act and its leading amendments command the support of all save a few of the surviving domestic Marxists. Antitrust litigation has created its own vested interest in the form of an industry which now provides a livelihood for hundreds of lawyers, economists, civil servants, and private detectives.

The steps by which the antitrust laws came to enjoy their present public support is a fascinating detective story. It can be read as showing the wise flexibility of the common law. It can also be read as showing our national capacity for deluding ourselves into thinking that we are controlling by legislation and judicial decision those

Virginia Law Review, 50 (1964), 413-434. Reprinted by permission of the publisher.

economic developments that are, in reality, the inevitable consequences of technological change, geography, the class struggle, and
pure chance. In this short Article, my concern is with one small
part of this story: how litigation under the Sherman Act has produced a theory of monopoly—or more accurately, a theory of competition—that guides the federal courts in their efforts to determine
what is lawful business practice. In a sense, the whole history of
antitrust policy can be read as the judicial quest for a working definition of competition; for before one can decide what the law of
monopoly ought to be, it is necessary to form a view of what the
process of competition is "really" like. . . .

Why did the reaction against *laissez faire* in the United States
produce antitrust while in most European countries it produced
strong socialist movements? I think it no accident that following
World War II the decline of the socialist tradition in the richer
countries of western Europe has been accompanied by a rise of
interest in antitrust. If "the commanding heights of industry" are
soon to be nationalized and operated as state-owned monopolies,
there is no point in worrying about the minor defects of a legal
framework that is shortly to be swept away. But if nationalization
and state monopoly is not the answer, then the revision of the existing legal framework can be a matter of importance. . . .

The important aspect of the corporate revolution is the manner
in which observers, especially judges, theorized about it after it
was largely over. The principal fruit of their reflection was the
distinction between "natural" and "unnatural" growth in the corporation. Corporate growth was natural provided that it was not
the result of wholesale mergers nor gained by the use of business
practices that were unfair. Such tactics could be either *mala in se*
(commercial bribery) or objectionable because they were the instrument of a sort of economic terror that discouraged competent rivals
from offering competition.

Tasks of Antitrust

The use of the merger to eliminate competition was explicitly
condemned by the Supreme Court for the first time in the *Northern
Secs. Co. v. United States,* and the condemnation was translated
into action by the dissolution of the power trust in 1911. In *United*

States v. Corn Prods. Ref. Co., divestiture of certain of the defendant's production facilities was ordered because he had sought to
maintain a market position by the use of tactics which the court
considered objectionable. In the opinion of Learned Hand, the
defendant's policy amounted to "candy without profit, syrup without profit, jam and jelly without profit—all to increase or maintain
the volume of business" [p. 988]. In the famous 1911 cases involving the oil and tobacco trusts, the Supreme Court was apparently
moved to order dissolution for two reasons that it did not bother to
distinguish. First, these two trusts had attained a near-monopoly
position (over eighty per cent of total output) in their respective
industries. Secondly, in each case, the near-monopoly position had
been secured with the aid of mergers and trade practices which
the Court believed to be unfair.

In the foregoing decisions we can discern the shadowy and elusive beginnings of the doctrine that monopolization per se is an
offense against the antitrust laws. In the cases noted above (with
the possible exception of the *Corn Products* decision), dissolution
and divestiture seem to have been ordered because the market
position of the defendant was found to be "unnatural" in that (a) its
size exceeded that needed for technically efficient production and
(b) its motive in growing so large had been desire for monopoly
profit. Thus, as of 1920, "to monopolize" was to obtain by merger
or "unfair" means a dominant market position which could not be
justified by the need for technically efficient production.

Nevertheless, in 1920 the course of antitrust litigation left unanswered two crucial questions: (1) what was the legal status of
a less-than-dominant market position that *could not* be justified by
the need for technically efficient production? (2) what was the
status of a dominant market position—say, seventy per cent or more
of the industry's output—that *could* be justified by an efficiency test?
For the last forty-four years, the courts have been striving to devise
an answer to the first question. They have never been disposed to
face squarely the second question; and cases seldom arise in a way
that requires them to face it squarely.

Economists have given the inelegant name of "oligopoly" to the
market occupied by a few sellers, none of which is dominant. And
the important cases which arise under section 2 of the Sherman
Act largely involve questions of what oligopolists may lawfully

do to advance their interests. They cannot of course "conspire" with
one another to increase their mutual profit by maintaining prices,
dividing markets, restricting output, or otherwise co-operating to
harass other rivals; any conspiracy leaves them open to a section 1
indictment. Yet, notwithstanding the now extensive body of case
law involving section 2 violations, it is exceedingly difficult to gen-
eralize about what oligopolists may lawfully do. That they may not
merge with one another seems to be settled law—at least they
hardly ever try to do so anymore. That they may not acquire small
competitors in the same "line of commerce in any section of the
country" is reasonably clear.

A few types of business practices have become virtually unlawful
per se when employed by oligopolists: contracts which tie the purchase of one product to another, exclusive dealing arrangements, or
the acquisition of a major supplier or customer. Beyond this point
generalization is difficult. The lack of coherence in the legal treatment of oligopolists makes lawyers unhappy because prediction of
judicial behavior is rendered more difficult. The economist is made
unhappy because he has trouble in discerning the economic objectives that the courts are seeking to achieve in their treatment of
oligopolists. . . .

My own feeling is that the confusion respecting what oligopolists
may lawfully do has two main sources. The first is the conservative
bias inevitable in any legal system worthy of the name. Thus the
court may properly refuse to permit the creation of market power
by a merger of independent firms; yet the court will not order the
destruction of comparable market power when it has, for many
years, been in the possession of an oligopolist. The blocking of an
undesirable merger precludes the defendant from securing economic benefits he does not yet have. Dissolution and divestiture
deprive him (assuming market power is reduced) of economic
benefits already enjoyed.

The second source of confusion in the law of oligopoly is the
difficulty in reconciling the condoned existence of oligopoly with
the condemnation of cartels in section 1 cases. One cannot ignore
the fact that a small number of sellers in a market may recognize
their stake by getting along with one another "up to a point" and
so avoiding mutually unprofitable price and sales combats. Consequently, oligopoly by its very existence must produce many of the

results that can only occur in industries which support a larger number of firms when a formal cartel is formed. Yet a formal cartel is pure criminal conspiracy under the interpretation of section 1 consistently affirmed by the federal courts. . . .

Many authorities have urged that the road to logical consistency lies through trust-busting on an unprecedented scale. One could, with equal truth, point out that such consistency may be achieved by a policy that legalizes cartels; but so great is our horror of formal cartels that this second alternative is scarcely ever noted. The usual recommendations are that mergers should be discouraged, oligopolies broken up, and, in some instances, new firms created by government loans and gifts ("artificial insemination") until firms are so numerous that the techniques of tacit collusion—price leadership, market sharing, etc.—become ineffective. The industry will then be, by definition, "workably" or "effectively" competitive.

In an industry which can only support a few efficient firms because there are substantial economies of scale, the economic cost of eliminating oligopoly is clear. If, in cases involving oligopoly, one looks at what the courts actually do in their decrees rather than at the language of their decisions, it is also clear that the courts are usually not prepared to pay this cost for the meager satisfaction of making antitrust policy logically consistent. The heart of antitrust is the resolve that oligopoly shall not evolve, or degenerate, into monopoly and that, if possible, it shall be pushed in the direction of workable competition by strictly controlling mergers and by placing handicaps on larger firms. This resolution imparts a rough consistency to the law of oligopoly; it also effectively subverts the application of per se tests to the behavior of oligopolists. What a firm may lawfully do to preserve or advance its interests depends upon a great many things—but mostly upon its absolute size and relative market share.

Competition as Process

Earlier in this paper I ventured the opinion that the whole history of antitrust policy in the United States can be viewed as the search for a working definition of competition. What is the progress of the quest . . . ? Some authorities would maintain that the answer to this question depends upon whether the reply comes from an economist or a lawyer. By one view, economists equate competition with impersonal price-making, the most impersonal being the "purest," whereas lawyers, in common with the generality of mankind, think of competition as rivalry among sellers to obtain labor, materials, and markets. My own feeling is that the differences in the thinking of economists and lawyers on the nature of competition are exaggerated and that both professions view competition as a process of challenge and response—"a sequence of moves and responses." As J. M. Clark has written:

> The attempt to excel may be called aggressive competition, in effect if not in intent; it may or may not be aimed at a particular rival's business. The attempt to equal a competitor's offer or minimize a rival's advantage is clearly defensive. Under competition the one implies the other, and it takes both kinds to make an effectively competitive situation— certainly in industry and trade and probably in agriculture. . . .
>
> Overlapping this, but not coextensive with it, is the distinction between moves of an initiatory character, including moves responding merely to the general situation in which a competitor finds himself, and responses precipitated by specific moves of a rival or rivals—responses of the nature of parries or ripostes. [Clark, *Competition as a Dynamic Process*, 14-15 (1961).]

Clark's conception of competition was not well received by many of his fellow economists, one frequent objection being that it is "too vague" and provides no handy set of rules by which one can determine whether a particular business "event," for example the merger in *Brown Shoe Co. v. United States,* is "competitive" or "monopolistic" in its consequences. . . .

Consider the oft-repeated charge that, on too many occasions, the courts have been unduly zealous in protecting competitors—especially small competitors—from the consequences of competition. The charge is certainly not without foundation. But the moral is not that judges use the antitrust laws to achieve the wrong end; rather it is that judges frequently exaggerate the importance to the preservation of competition of the small competitors threatened with extinction. Admittedly judges can get their facts wrong. . . . the fact remains that, in certain instances—for example in the automobile industry today—competition can only be preserved by insuring the survival of established competitors. In these situations, the courts can only preserve certain features of the competitive process by sacrificing others. Under ideal conditions, competition guarantees a choice of suppliers to consumers, economic opportunity for aspiring businessmen, and efficient production. When the market can support only one efficient producer, conditions are obviously not ideal.

Since no succinct definition of the competitive process is possible, experts may differ widely on the wisdom of any particular antitrust decision. Here one can only say the obvious. The first requirement of competition is competitors; but a policy that preserves or creates competitors is subject to diminishing returns. If, in the automobile industry, the object is competition among domestic manufacturers, two competitors are indispensable, and four are probably better than two. It is not clear that eight are better than seven. . . . Whenever the wisdom of a particular antitrust decision is appraised in law journals—allegedly the court of last resort—three closely related questions are in order. The first is whether the decision is calculated to preserve any essential feature of the competitive process. Assuming an affirmative answer to this question, one ought next to ask: what costs must be incurred to secure the protection of "competition" ordered by the court? Finally, are these costs excessive? . . .

After all, whereas the economic benefits of a policy of economic decentralization enforced by law are quite nebulous, the economic costs of such a policy are quite specific. One cannot "prove" that antitrust policy serves to accelerate the rate of economic progress or improve the distribution of economic resources. But one can make a virtually irrefutable case that certain economic wastes—the heavy advertising budgets of automobile firms, frequent automobile style changes, cross-hauling in steel, and the reluctance of efficient firms (for example, the Great Atlantic & Pacific Tea Company) to expand—are traceable to our policy of discouraging cartels and mergers.

The disturbing truth—disturbing to an economist at any rate—is that the usual case for antitrust policy rests upon assumptions that he must either question in his professional capacity or accept largely on faith as a layman. Economists can without difficulty demonstrate that in the steel industry a cartel could market the product more efficiently than the present oligopoly. (Most steel executives probably know this instinctively.) But no sensible economist believes that he has any special competence to say what would happen to the rate of productivity increase in the steel industry over the next thirty years if the industry were permitted to transform itself into a tight cartel. In popular discussions the productivity achievements of the American economy are often attributed, in whole or in part, to the success of the antitrust laws in preserving competition. This attribution is a particularly egregious example of the fallacy of association. Economic systems with markedly different legal frameworks have done as well and, for some intervals of time, even better. . . .

The Uncertain Economic Case for Antitrust

The foregoing observations have implied that many, if not most, economists now view with skepticism the most important of the economic arguments that are usually employed to justify antitrust policy. . . . Probably only those economists who follow day-to-day developments in antitrust realize how far the erosion of the faith has gone. After American economists were converted from their faith in the "invisible hand" to a belief in the necessity of antitrust, four arguments came to enjoy nearly universal acceptance. In the absence of intervention by the state:

1. Large firms will be created by merger. They will then employ "unfair" tactics to eliminate equally efficient small rivals who could have survived in a fair fight. Having gained the fields for themselves, large firms will employ the threat of this "predatory" competition to discourage the entry of new rivals.
2. In many industries, cartels will emerge and succeed in persuading members to restrict output in the interest of higher profits.
3. The misallocation of resources arising from the pricing of cartels and the "monopoly power" inherent in a dominant market position protected by "unfair" means is statistically important.
4. In most industries the rate of productivity increase will be slowed down by the emergence of monopoly; for it is the fear of innovating rivals that drives a firm to keep abreast of the latest developments in technology and to undertake research and development on its own.

In recent years the arm-chair reflection and empirical work of economists have combined to cast doubt on the validity of three of these four arguments. It can be demonstrated that there is no advantage in getting rid of a business rival by unfair competition unless the survivor can take over his market share and hold it for some interval before a new rival is drawn in by his excess profit. But if any market power, once gained, can be peacefully held for a time, rational business behavior dictates that you buy out the business rival or merge with him. This way the losses imposed on both parties by "excessive" price cutting can be avoided. Moreover, in recent years careful analysis has shown that exclusive dealing, full-line forcing, and tying contracts—trade practices which were once thought to be the epitome of unfair competition—are for the most part innocuous. In most cases their object and effect is not to exclude rivals from the market but merely to increase profits by charging different prices in different markets.

Two efforts have been made to measure "the costs of industrial monopoly"; both have found them to be negligible—to amount to less than one per cent of national income. (It should be mentioned that neither of these studies dealt with the costs of monopoly arising from public regulation of business, and there is still an excellent prima facie case that the sums exacted from consumers by regulated industries are by no means negligible.) . . .

The argument that cartels are undesirable because they misallocate resources is still accepted with varying degrees of reservation by most economists. In theory, there is misallocation of resources to the extent that cartel power is used to raise price above marginal cost; it is assumed that the "social value" of the product is measured by price while "social cost"—the value of goods and services that must be sacrificed to produce the product—is measured by its marginal cost. This argument, however, no longer carries its former weight. Case studies of cartels in action have not revealed them to be very powerful organizations. Indeed, several economists have concluded that so long as the state does not impose controls on entry into an industry which contains a fairly large number of firms, the possibility of cheating and fear of new firms will keep the cartel price close to the competitive price.

When firms are few and entry is difficult (automobiles, aluminum, heavy electrical equipment), it is reasonable to assume that a cartel can raise prices. But unhappily, in such a situation, there is no way that production can be efficiently organized without a cartel. For efficient production requires that output be distributed among the firms in the industry in a way that minimizes total costs, and a distribution of output that minimizes total cost cannot be secured without the use of quotas and the pooling of profits that necessitate a resort to the cartel. In the steel industry, for example, the wastes of cross-hauling occur because sellers are not allowed to pool orders, fill each order from the plant located nearest to the customer, and then divide profits. . . .

IN DEFENSE OF THE COURTS

The problem faced by the courts in devising an operational theory of competition is crudely analogous to that of any person charged with the task of overseeing a competitive sport. The game should be played competently and vigorously with rewards to those who deserve them, but the game should go on. Overseeing a competitive sport requires, of course, that rules should be made and enforced. But it also requires that rules should be changed if and when the continued success of certain players threatens the future of the sport itself. In the absence of rule changes or periodic confiscation of the winner's earnings, competitive games do tend to break down. In the case of the business game, antitrust policy decrees that the game shall be played according to a set of rules that seeks to insure, *inter alia,* that the prizes are distributed according to merit: consumers get the goods and services that they want—or at any rate, that they are prepared to pay for—and the most efficient producers provide those goods and services. But antitrust policy must also insure that the process of competition will not be jeopardized by the success of the ablest—or luckiest—competitors.

Unhappily, there seems to be a silent conspiracy to obscure the important issues of antitrust policy by denying that the success of *competition* and the success of competitors are conflicting objectives. The supporters of antitrust will not concede that monopoly can be the product of superior efficiency or superior luck. Defendants in antitrust cases will seldom admit that their situation is anything but competitive. And our legal tradition requires that judges in antitrust cases shall pay lip-service to the myth that they are merely "applying the law."

If one assumes that, given *laissez faire,* the scale of efficient production is so low relative to market demand that no producers can long maintain a profitable market position, then there is no conflict of policy objectives. The game is perforce self-perpetuating, and there is really no need for an antitrust policy. Almost no American economist would today assert that *laissez faire* is a guarantee that the process of competition *in its present form* will persist in industries where it is presently found. Whether the new market situations that a policy of *laissez faire* would soon bring about would qualify as "competition" is a question for semanticists. What is "inter-industry competition" to one man is "late-stage monopoly capitalism" to another. The history of mergers in this country and abroad provides conclusive evidence that a policy of *laissez faire* can be remarkably effective in reducing the number of firms in the manufacturing and financial sectors of the economy. . . .

MONOPOLIZATION AS A PER SE OFFENSE

We might state the gravamen of the preceding discussion in this way. To say that the object of the antitrust laws is the protection of something called "competition" is at best unenlightening and at worst misleading. For over thirty years Professor Edward Chamberlin has protested in vain against the nearly universal view that there exists a spectrum of business situations with "pure" competition at one end and "monopoly" at the other. Instead he has maintained that "most economic situations are composites of both competition and monopoly, and that, whenever this is the case, a false view is given by neglecting either one of the two forces and regarding the situation as made up entirely (even though imperfectly) of the other." Chamberlin achieved fame with his theory of "monopolistic competition," but his objection to the use of the spectrum was largely ignored. The modern fashion in both economics and law is to treat every business situation as falling somewhere between the poles of the spectrum. The truth is that competition is a process and, as such, can be described but not defined. One might as well try to define "economic activity"—indeed the two terms are nearly interchangeable when used to describe the way in which production and distribution are organized in an economy characterized by an elaborate division of labor and the use of markets.

It would be more accurate to say that the object of antitrust

policy is the protection of certain features of competition viewed
as a process. But even this statement is not very satisfactory. The
desirability of protecting any particular feature of competition—
say the existence of at least three firms in the automobile industry
—cannot be ascertained unless some estimate is made of the economic "cost" of conferring this protection. Federal judges are, of
course, perfectly aware that their antitrust decisions have costs. But
while we have every reason to believe that these costs are weighed
most carefully, the reckoning is seldom done openly. The ritual of
the adversary process wonderfully conceals the manner in which
the important economic issues are "really" clarified and disposed of
in antitrust cases. Thus it almost never happens that the court will
refuse the Government's request for dissolution or divestiture on
the ground that the efficiency of the dismembered enterprise would
suffer. Yet does anyone doubt that the probable effect of trust-
busting on business efficiency is the central economic issue in every
case where the Government seeks dissolution or divestiture?

Since the courts cannot ignore the economic consequences of
their decisions in important antitrust cases, they have been extremely reluctant to devise per se rules in section 2 cases. One can
even argue that there is no set of per se rules applicable to section 2
cases—only strong presumptions—and that every movement in the
direction of complete predictability in section 2 litigation meets,
sooner or later, with the check that compels resort to some reasonableness test. . . .

The theory that some specific share of the market can constitute
a per se violation of section 2 is most likely to be put to test in the
automobile industry, where General Motors—already in possession
of over fifty per cent of passenger car production—must display
considerable ingenuity to see that its share of the market does not
increase with unseemly rapidity.

I think it very possible, even probable, that sometime within the
next twenty years, General Motors will be broken up as a result
of antitrust litigation. But if dissolution is ordered, it will be because
the courts have decided that, in the automobile industry, the gains
of decentralization will exceed those economies of large scale production that must be sacrificed to achieve them. And this proposition will hold even though dissolution is ostensibly ordered be-

cause General Motors' share of automobile output constitutes a per se violation of section 2. . . .

The two main goals of antitrust policy are generally taken to be decentralized decision-making in the business world and economic efficiency. Often one of these goals must be sacrificed to achieve the other. The necessity of making this choice has largely prevented the development of per se rules in section 2 cases. So long as federal judges are reasonable men par excellence, it will continue to do so. The structure and performance of important sections of the American economy are simply too important to be left to per se rules. . . .

PART II

The Merger Controversy

MERGERS AND THE NEW ANTITRUST POLICY

Jesse W. Markham

Jesse W. Markham is Professor of Economics at Princeton University. He is the author of numerous antitrust articles and is a former Chief Economist for the Federal Trade Commission.

Probably the most dramatic change of the postwar period in the institutional environment of the business firm is the renewed vigor and vigilance that has been injected into antitrust policy. The change is dramatic in part because it was unexpected. . . . The trust-busting days of President Theodore Roosevelt, and later of Thurman Arnold, differed from the decade of virtual antitrust suspension in the 1920s only in the sense that in the former more—but not a great many more—near-monopolies were prosecuted. Accordingly, the business community, the legal profession, economists, even the antitrust agencies themselves, could with reasonable safety assume that antitrust policy now and in the foreseeable future would be approximately what it always had been, a loose prohibition on the possession of—or, more accurately, the flagrant abuse of—undisputed monopoly power and a tight prohibition on price-fixing and related agreements among competitors.

This prohibition left open broad avenues of corporate growth. Until the 1940s and the *Alcoa* decision there existed virtually no antitrust constraint on *internal* growth. The firm could not, of course,

Originally published under the title of "The New Antitrust Policy and the Individual Business Firm" in *Law and Contemporary Problems*, XXX (1965), 607ff. Copyright, 1965, Duke University.

grow by illegal means such as predatory or discriminatory pricing or other unfair methods of competition, but there was no bar to firm growth by means considered "honestly industrial." Antitrust policy also permitted almost all growth by acquisition short of creating a virtual monopoly; the doctrine enunciated in *U.S. Steel* that "mere size is no offense" not only left the permissible limits of growth by merger at least as high as sixty per cent of the market, it provided an opening for the building of large organizations through the conglomerate merger of firms already in possession of larger market shares. With the Sherman Act prohibiting only a few of the most obvious consolidations for monopoly and the Clayton Act applicable only to stock acquisitions, firms could grow at will through asset acquisitions and were not seriously limited in their growth through stock acquisitions. . . .

While the role mergers have played in company growth, and in the disparate rates of growth among individual firms, is subject to some controversy, there is general agreement that it has been significant. One of the few extensive quantitative studies in this area shows that about eighty large corporations owe from one-third to one-quarter of their size to past mergers and acquisitions; one distinguished and highly reputable economist in reviewing the study offered persuasive reasons for concluding that the fraction is significantly higher and that "merger has been the basic method by which individual firms have acquired high shares in major industries in the United States."

Against this background the "new" antitrust policy adds up to a dramatic change in the permissible means of firm growth. The most significant aspects of the new policy are (1) the rapidity with which it has been expanded to encompass business practices heretofore assumed to be the normal and natural modes of business conduct, and (2) the greatly increased vigor with which it has been administered against practices nominally considered of questionable legality but for the most part seldom challenged. Moreover, the new policy, viewed prospectively, has a completely new ingredient. At the same time that both old and recently amended statutes are being administered far more vigorously than at any previous period in history, a concomitant of which is the emergence of several new judicial doctrines every year, congressional committees are introduc-

ing new and decidedly more proscriptive legislation in each session
of Congress. . . .

I
THE SPECIFIC COMPONENTS
OF THE NEW ANTITRUST POLICY

In precise terms, what are the once "normal" business practices
the new antitrust policy now prohibits? While the individual decisions cover a wide variety of business situations each of which in
some respect differs from the others, taken together they reflect
the Government's serious concern over the large size of corporations making up the business community and what the Government
appears to regard as a corollary, a serious concern over preserving
the existing population of small business enterprises. The legality of
a business activity is, as will be shown below, no longer determined
solely on the basis of its competitive effects—the traditional standard—but may be determined on the basis of how it affects the number, size, and immediate and prospective opportunities of small
firms which may be in actual or potential competition with the
larger firms involved in the case.

The component of the new antitrust policy is most clearly seen
in some of the recent merger decisions. In the *Brown Shoe* case, the
Supreme Court held the merger of Brown Shoe, the fourth largest
shoe manufacturer with four per cent of total shoe production, and
Kinney (the desired acquisition), a large family-style shoe retail
chain accounting for 1.6 per cent of retail shoe sales, to be illegal
on the grounds that (1) "numerous independent retailers" would
be disadvantaged through the economies of production, distribution, and style alterations that strong national chains could effect,
and (2) independent shoe manufacturers would be foreclosed from
Kinney stores as outlets for their shoes. These particulars were not
as important, however, as Chief Justice Warren's statement of what
he thought to be the broad purpose of section 7 of the Clayton Act,
as amended:

The dominant theme pervading congressional consideration of the 1950
amendments was a fear of what was considered to be a rising tide of

economic concentration in the American economy. . . . Other considerations cited in support of the bill were the desirability of retaining "local
control" over industry and the protection of small businesses. (pp. 315-
316).

One of the very important problems recent merger decisions
create for business firms are the multiple and conflicting standards
they lay down. Chief Justice Warren, continuing in *Brown Shoe,*
asserted,

It is competition, not competitors, which the [Clayton] Act protects. But
we cannot fail to recognize Congress' desire to promote competition
through the protection of viable, small, locally owned businesses. Congress appreciated that occasional higher costs and prices might result
from the maintenance of fragmented industries and markets. It resolved
these competing considerations in favor of decentralization. (p. 344)

As two veteran students of antitrust have remarked,

No matter how many times you read it, that passage states: Although
mergers are not rendered unlawful by the mere fact that small independent stores may be adversely affected, we must recognize that mergers
are unlawful when small independent stores may be adversely affected.

The decision-making bodies of large business firms may be justifiably perplexed over just exactly what the language of *Brown Shoe*
permits and what it prohibits, but they can scarcely be in doubt as
to what the ultimate decision in fact was: A merger that might disadvantage small independent shoe manufacturers or retailers, even
if it leads to lower prices and lower costs, violates section 7.

The Federal Trade Commission declared Procter & Gamble's
acquisition of Clorox to be in contravention of Clayton Act section 7
on the grounds that the combination, with Proctor & Gamble's great
advertising and capital resources behind the established name of
Clorox, would increase its share of the liquid bleach market at the
expense of the numerous small liquid bleach producers.

The Federal Trade Commission decided the *Foremost Dairies* case
on similar grounds. In ordering Foremost to divest itself of dairies
it had acquired in ten particular local markets the Commission
noted that section 7 "was designed to prevent one company or a

group of companies from using mergers to distort irrevocably market structures in small business industries." Early in its opinion the Commission conceded that many factors—technological changes, new public health standards, the bonding of milk plants, federal and state market orders, the advantages of "hedging" through expansion into new geographical areas and product lines—all favored the large processor and added up to strong economic incentives for existing firms to grow in size, even to grow by merger. But these market incentives to grow were subject to the constraining forces of section 7, and these forces were directed toward the preservation of small business.

A number of recent cases reiterate the doctrine laid down in *Brown Shoe*, *Procter & Gamble*, and *Foremost Dairies*. Significantly, this doctrine seems to rest far more on the statements of individual senators and congressmen made in the course of floor debates on the Celler-Kefauver Amendment, and on those contained in various reports and studies cited by participants in the debates, than on the language of amended section 7 itself as finally enacted. It is not surprising that more than a modest sprinkling of these statements extol the social beneficence of decentralized industry under "local" ownership, *i.e.*, small business, and that the actual and potential maleficence of industrial concentration, absentee ownership, and oligopoly are all easily equated with big business. Hence, once the Court has accorded such statements the status of competent authority, it has been a relatively easy matter to recompose section 7 as enacted into the less restrictive language of the floor debates.

There has thus emerged the doctrine that even though a given merger may not have demonstrably been shown to have the probable effect of substantially lessening competition, it may by some "ultimate reckoning of social or economic debits and credits" be injurious to "social" competition, to be distinguished from "market" competition. In two even more recent cases decided by the Supreme Court section 7 was extended in scope to areas hitherto regarded as beyond its reach, as the Court turned aside the "ultimate reckoning" doctrine when made by the defense. In the *Philadelphia Nat'l Bank* case the Court extended the jurisdiction of section 7 to include commercial banking. In doing so it also laid down the doctrine that even though a merger might possibly produce a net *increase* in competition when all markets were considered, it was

nevertheless illegal if it tended to lessen competition in one of the
relevant markets, sub-markets, or lines of commerce. As Justice
Brennan put it,

We are clear, however, that a merger the effect of which "may be substantially to lessen competition" is not saved because, on some ultimate
reckoning of social or economic debits and credits, it may be deemed
beneficial. A value choice of such magnitude is beyond the ordinary
limits of judicial competence. . . . (p. 371)

It would seem reasonably clear that the Court could find a merger
bringing together thirty per cent of a relevant market in contravention of section 7 without referral to the ultimate reckoning doctrine at all. In rejecting it as an inappropriate standard after having
resorted to it frequently in immediately preceding cases to support
judgments denouncing the merger at hand, and less than a year later
going a long way toward returning to it again in *Continental Can*,
the Court has greatly enlarged the area of potential illegality while
substantially reducing the acquiring firm's means of defense. In the
recent *Penn-Olin* case, the Court extended section 7 to *internal*
growth when accomplished through the instrument of a joint venture. The joint construction of a sodium chlorate plant by Pennsalt
Chemical and Olin Mathieson would have been illegal if it had been
shown that either joint venturer would have entered the new market independently if the joint venture had not been formed.

The recently enunciated doctrines are not limited to Clayton Act
section 7 decisions since these decisions have undoubtedly affected
those rendered under the Sherman Act. In *United States v. First
Nat'l Bank of Lexington,* the Supreme Court found that the merger
of two competing banks was itself a violation of section 1 of the
Sherman Act. Indeed, the majority opinion of Justice Douglas goes
a long way toward making such mergers *per se* illegal and having
about the same legal status as price-fixing agreements. And in cases
brought against American Optical Company and Bausch & Lomb,
Inc., the Government is entering a prayer that each of the defendants be required to divest itself of all their more than 400 wholesale
branches throughout the country and perpetually enjoined from
engaging in wholesaling or in business as dispensing opticians. The
argument is that these channels of commerce are now "foreclosed"

from the independent manufacturers of lenses, frames, and other ophthalmic materials and equipment and that defendants have a competitive advantage over the more than 600 independent wholesale laboratories.

The contrast between these recent antitrust doctrines and that laid down by the Court in the *Columbia Steel* case is striking. In that case the Court held that it could not forbid U.S. Steel from accomplishing through acquisition that which it could clearly accomplish legally through internal expansion. The recently enunciated section 7 and Sherman Act doctrines have completely overturned the *Columbia* doctrine. It is equally obvious that they have completely demolished what the *Alcoa* decision may possibly have left of the *U.S. Steel* doctrine that "mere size is no offense." . . .

II
THE IMPACT OF THE NEW ANTITRUST ON BUSINESS FIRMS

The foregoing decisions and proposed legislation obviously add up to a substantial change in antitrust policy, a change that holds important implications for corporate enterprise, big and small. It is now perfectly clear that the large corporation, confronting such doctrines as those laid down in *Alcoa, Brown Shoe, Procter & Gamble, Foremost Dairies, Philadelphia Nat'l Bank,* and *Penn-Olin* must carefully select its means of growth. The merger decisions could possibly be turned against almost any expansion by large firms through acquisition, and *Alcoa* and *Penn-Olin* limit the means and direction of internal growth. Pending legislation, if enacted, would not only limit much more drastically the growth and size of business firms in the future but would reduce the present size of many large corporations.

In view of the contemporary corporation's propensity to expand through merger it is clear that the newly enunciated doctrines can significantly affect the conduct of corporate affairs. Between 1951 and 1961, the 500 largest industrial firms made 3,404 acquisitions, an average of 6.8 acquisitions per firm. Between 1948 and 1964, at least 720 manufacturing firms having assets of $10 million and over, in total accounting for $23 billion in assets, were acquired by other firms. The assets acquired in the $10 million-$25 million asset-size

class represented 40.3 per cent of the total manufacturing assets in
that size class in 1959. The corresponding proportion of total assets
acquired through merger for the $25 million-$50 million class was
38.1 per cent; for the $50 million-$100 million class, 26.7 per cent;
for the $100 million-$250 million class, 14.2 per cent; and for the
over $250 million class, 0.5 per cent. Stated in terms of simple mem-
bers, every fifteen years or so about one-quarter of all the manufacturing firms in the $50 million-$250 million asset-size class, and
nearly half of those falling in the $10 million-$50 million asset-size
class, are merged with other manufacturing firms. Merger is clearly
a frequent occurrence among corporate enterprise, both as a means
of growth and, since for every buyer there is a seller, as a means
of terminating independent corporate existence. While these data
serve amply to document the fact that industrial mergers still go on
apace, they also measure the extent to which corporate enterprise
may have to alter their business conduct in the future.

The new antitrust policy is not limited to future acquisitions. As
former Assistant Attorney General William Orrick has emphasized,
those that have not yet been challenged are subject to being challenged at any future time. As he stated before the Antitrust Section
of the ABA in 1964, "Surely there is nothing revolutionary in the
concept that earlier acquisitions may be questioned at a much later
date." He pointed to *Standard Oil* and *DuPont-General Motors* as
examples from the past, and to pending cases against Monsanto,
The Blue Chip Stamp Co., Valley National Bank of Arizona, American Smelting and Refining Company, Richfield Oil Company, and
the Newmont Mining Corporation as examples in the present. He
could have included on the list the case now pending against General Motors for its acquisition of Euclid in 1953. Since it has been
calculated that most large corporations owe about one-third of their
present size to past acquisitions and mergers, it is clear that such
corporations are potentially susceptible to dissolution under section
7 at any time. This vulnerability puts the present-day large corporation in a much different position with respect to antitrust policy
than its predecessors.

The most significant impact of the more intensified antitrust
policy, however, must probably be measured in terms of its present
and future effects on corporate decisions concerning growth rather
than in terms of specific acquisitions arrested in specific litigations.

Antitrust law, probably more than most law, has its principal effect through compliance. The many open forums of the legal and economics professions dedicated to "the current status of antitrust policy" keep the more alert members of the business community, or at least their legal counsel, well informed on what the statutes proscribe. The legal means of growth are known to have been greatly restricted since the 1948 *Columbia Steel* decision in which the Supreme Court stated that it could not keep U.S. Steel from acquiring through merger that which it was perfectly free to construct for itself. It can be assumed that most large corporations now make expansion plans under the known constraints the new antitrust policy imposes. The fact that the number of cases is still high only reflects the fast moving pace at which the new doctrines have developed; most of the pending cases probably would not have materialized had the decisions on the "deep pocket," "ultimate reckoning," and "foreclosure" doctrines been passed down earlier.

It is now reasonably clear that any horizontal merger involving eight to ten per cent or more of a relevant line of commerce and that any vertical or "conglomerate" acquisition by a large corporation of a small firm having small competitors is highly vulnerable. Former Assistant Attorney General Orrick stated in a speech on May 12, 1964, that most important horizontal mergers may now be considered illegal *per se*. Nor can the acquiring firm sustain its acquisition (1) by showing that the *net* effect of the merger may be to increase competition, even though in a specific more narrowly defined market competition may be lessened; (2) by showing that the merger permits it more effectively to compete with a larger rival in a "dominant" position; or (3) that the merger promotes efficiency and is a normal response to market and technological forces. It is not as clear what mergers *are* legal, but presumably mergers among small corporations and vertical and conglomerate acquisitions by firms smaller than most of the acquired firm's rival's avoid most of the recently developed doctrines.

The new doctrines raise important questions of public policy to which there are no obvious answers. Thoughtful scholars and competent students of economic policy have questioned the wisdom of providing aid and protection to small business through the antitrust laws rather than the traditional small business institutions; the wisdom of forbidding cost-reducing and technologically inspired

mergers at such low levels of concentration as were involved in
Brown Shoe and *Foremost Dairies;* and the wisdom of choking off
so many of the avenues of corporate growth only a short decade
ago regarded by the business community as routine.

On the other hand, the new antitrust policy seems to bid fair
eventually to reduce the level of over-all concentration as well as
the level of concentration in specific lines of commerce; both results
have been regarded by many as desirable since the enactment of
the Sherman Act. . . . But more than this, the new policy will force
individual corporations to consider more seriously the alternatives
to the acquisition of domestic companies as means of company
growth and product diversification. For the large corporation on
which antitrust policy has been turned, the logical alternative to
such domestic acquisitions is the acquisition of foreign companies,
especially in western Europe. In fact, in the six-year period 1958-63
United States manufacturing corporations established at least 2,200
"new operations" in Europe; since more than three-quarters of the
total were located in the European Common Market countries, they
were very likely made in response to the formation of the European
Economic Community rather than to the new legal prohibitions on
domestic mergers and acquisitions. The total represents a sample
of both newly established and acquired facilities. Acquisitions are
not shown separately and are not identified by acquiring firms, but
the data suggest that the larger United States corporations probably
acquired more foreign than domestic firms during this period. . . .

The more stringent new section 7 doctrines will also require that
large corporations substitute new plant construction for some acquisitions they would otherwise make. Indeed, this will very likely
be socially the most beneficial effect of the new antitrust policy.
Generally, all other things remaining the same, large firms will
grow more rapidly when permitted to acquire going establishments
than if this avenue of growth is denied them, since product extension through construction of new plants involves greater risks and
higher orders of uncertainty than the acquisition of going organizations. On the other hand, new plant construction comprises a net
addition to the economy's total productive capacity whereas an
acquisition, at least in the initial instance, simply transfers the
ownership of existing capacity. However, the ultimate effect of a
more stringent ban on acquisition cannot be so easily predicted;

when large corporations make acquisitions they generally expand the acquired firm's capacity through new plant construction. Hence, a vigorous antimerger policy encourages the substitution of some new plant construction for acquisition and at the same time discourages new plant additions to acquired firms.

The economic calculus is clearly not capable of predicting the economic impact of our new antitrust policy with any high order of precision. The new doctrines have been laid down so rapidly and so recently that they have not perceptibly affected the principal economic indicators to which they are related—not even the indexes of over-all merger activity. Yet it is clear that they hold significant implications for the future conduct of the economic affairs of large corporations and will, unless reversed, force the large multiproduct corporation to explore new alternatives to merger and acquisition. The big issue, of course, is what logically should be the specific objectives of antitrust policy and at what price should they be bought. This question is not likely to be resolved. . . .

MERGERS AND THE COURTS

Edited by Richard E. Low

The weaving together of economics and law is well illustrated by the handling of merger cases by the courts. The following extracts from judicial opinions speak for themselves in the areas of antitrust objectives, market boundaries and affirmative defenses for mergers. The reader should note that a (U.S.) citation means the Supreme Court, a (F. 2d) citation means a federal court of appeals and a (F. Supp.) citation means a federal district court.

I. OBJECTIVES OF SECTION 7

1. Preventing Increased Economic Concentration

From this country's beginning there has been an abiding and widespread fear of the evils which flow from monopoly—that is the concentration of economic power in the hands of a few. On the basis of this fear, Congress in 1890, when many of the Nation's industries were already concentrated into what it deemed too few hands, passed the Sherman Act in an attempt to prevent further concentration and to preserve competition among a large number of sellers. . . .

The Sherman Act failed to protect the smaller businessmen from elimination through the monopolistic pressures of large combinations which used mergers to grow ever more powerful. As a result in 1914 Congress, viewing mergers as a continuous, pervasive threat to small business, passed § 7 of the Clayton Act which prohibited corporations under most circumstances from merging by purchasing the stock of their competitors. . . .

Like the Sherman Act in 1890 and the Clayton Act in 1914, the

basic purpose of the 1950 Celler-Kefauver Act was to prevent economic concentration in the American economy by keeping a large
number of small competitors in business. In stating the purposes of
their bill, both of its sponsors, Representative Celler and Senator
Kefauver, emphasized their fear, widely shared by other members
of Congress, that this concentration was rapidly driving the small
businessman out of the market. The period from 1940 to 1947, which
was at the center of attention throughout the hearings and debates
on the Celler-Kefauver bill, has been characterized by a series of
mergers between large corporations and their smaller competitors
resulting in the steady erosion of the small independent business
in our economy. [*U.S.* v. *Von's Grocery Co.*, 384 U.S. 270, 274-277
(1966)]

   Much of the fuel for the congressional debates on concentration
in the American economy was derived from a contemporary study
by the Federal Trade Commission on corporate acquisitions between 1940 and 1947. See Report of the Federal Trade Commission
on the Merger Movement: A Summary Report (1948). A critical
study of the FTC report, published while the 1950 amendment was
pending in Congress, concluded that the effect of the recent merger
movement on concentration had been slight. Lintner & Butters, Effect
of Mergers on Industrial Concentration, 1940-1947, 32 Rev. of Econ.
& Statistics 30 (1950). Two economists for the Federal Trade Commission later acquiesced in that conclusion. Blair & Houghton, The
Lintner-Butters Analysis of the Effect of Mergers on Industrial Concentration 1940-1947, 33 Rev. of Econ. & Statistics 63, 67, n. 12 (1951).
[*Ibid.*, 284, n. 6 (Mr. Justice Stewart, dissenting)]

   In fact, if our economic system of free enterprise is to survive, it
is probably necessary for the Government to interpose itself in those
situations where the natural force of economic rivalry tends toward
undue concentration. Those who believe in Marxian economics,
believe that the tendency toward monopoly is inevitable. It is to
withstand these economic pressures that Congress has enacted the
antitrust laws. [*U.S.* v. *Kennecott Copper Corp.*, 231 F. Supp. 95, 103
(S.D.N.Y., 1964)] Congress has not mandated the Commission or
the courts "to campaign against 'superconcentration' in the absence
of any evidence of harm to competition." [*FTC* v. *Procter & Gamble
Co.*, U.S. Law Week, Advanced Opinions, #343, B1445, 1967 (Mr.
Justice Harlan, concurring)]

2. The Incipiency Doctrine

Congress sought to preserve competition among many small businesses by arresting a trend toward concentration in its incipiency before that trend developed to the point that a market was left in the grip of a few big companies. [*U.S.* v. *Von's Grocery Co.,* 384 U.S. 270, 277 (1966)]

Section 7 of the Clayton Act was intended to arrest the anticompetitive effects of market power in their incipiency. The core question is whether a merger may substantially lessen competition, and necessarily requires a prediction of the merger's impact on competition, present and future. The section can deal only with probabilities, not with certainties. And there is certainly no requirement that the anticompetitive power manifest itself in anticompetitive action before § 7 can be called into play. If the enforcement of § 7 turned on the existence of actual anticompetitive practices, the congressional policy of thwarting such practices in their incipiency would be frustrated. [*FTC* v. *Procter & Gamble Co.,* U.S. Law Week, Advanced Opinions, #343, B1436 (1967)]

3. Protecting Competition v. Protecting Competitors

If ever such a merger would not violate § 7, certainly it does when it takes place in a market characterized by a long and continuous trend toward fewer and fewer owner-competitors which is exactly the sort of trend which Congress, with power to do so, declared must be arrested. [*U.S.* v. *Von's Grocery Co.,* 384 U.S. 270, 278 (1966)]

. . . the purpose of § 7 is to protect competition, not to protect competitors, and every § 7 case must be decided in the light of that clear statutory purpose. Today the Court turns its back on these two basic principles and on all the decisions that have followed them.

The Court makes no effort to appraise the competitive effects of this acquisition in terms of the contemporary economy of the retail food industry in the Los Angeles area. Instead, through a simple exercise in sums, it finds that the number of individual competitors in the market has decreased over the years, and, apparently on the theory that the degree of competition is invariably proportional to the number of competitors, it holds that this historic reduction in the number of competing units is enough under § 7 to invalidate a merger within the market, with no need to examine the economic concentration of the market, the level of competition in the market, or the potential adverse effect of the merger on that competition. This startling *per se* rule is contrary not only to our previous decisions, but contrary to the language of § 7, contrary to the legislative history of the 1950 amendment, and contrary to economic reality. [*Ibid.*, 282-283 (Mr. Justice Stewart, dissenting)]

4. Efficiency?

Possible economies cannot be used as a defense to illegality. Congress was aware that some mergers which lessen competition may also result in economies but it struck the balance in favor of protecting competition. [*FTC* v. *Procter & Gamble,* U.S. Law Week, Advanced Opinions, #343, B1439 (1967)]

Congress rejected the alleged advantages of size in favor of the preservation of a competitive system. The consideration to be accorded to benefits of one kind or another in one section or another of the country which may flow from a merger involving a substantial lessening of competition is a matter properly to be urged upon Congress. It is outside the province of the Court. [*U.S.* v. *Bethlehem Steel Corporation,* 168 F. Supp. 576, 617-618 (S.D.N.Y. 1958)]

The economic forces which lead to amalgamation and integration of large industries are very real forces. They may indeed be desirable forces. They often lead to economic and efficient operation. It is no answer to say that such processes are desirable from an economic standpoint, for Congress has said that the tendency is undesirable from a social standpoint, and we must enforce the law as Congress wrote it and as Congress intended that it be enforced. [*U.S.* v. *Kennecott Copper Corp.,* 231 F. Supp. 95, 103 (S.D.N.Y. 1964)]

The problem of efficiencies . . . must still be faced. The Court attempts to brush the question aside by asserting that Congress preferred competition to economies, but neglects to determine whether certain economies are inherent in the idea of competition. If it is conceded, as it must be, that Congress had reasons for favoring competition, then more efficient operation must have been among them. . . . Economies achieved by one firm may stimulate matching innovation by others, the very essence of competition. They always allow the total output to be delivered to the consumer with an expenditure of fewer resources. . . . The responsible agency should examine and weigh possible efficiencies arising from the merger in order to determine whether, on balance, competition has been substantially lessened. [*FTC* v. *Procter & Gamble,* U.S. Law Week, Advanced Opinions, #343, B1459 (1967), Mr. Justice Harlan, concurring]

II. MARKETS, PRODUCTS AND ECONOMIC THEORY

1. Cross-elasticity of Demand

The defendant, relying on the testimony of some brokers that customers in placing orders often specify either beet or cane, insists that the two products are not fully competitive. And in further support of this contention, it points to the finding that cane normally sells at 20¢ per cwt. higher than beet. However, substantial evidence traces the differential in part to the early history of the industry, when the higher purity of cane allowed it to command a higher rate, and, in part, to the packaging and trademarks used in the merchandising of cane sugar for the household consumer market. There was some evidence that in certain areas the differential no longer exists: especially is that so in the industrial market. And there was evidence that a change in the price of one produces an equivalent and corresponding change in the price of the other. Sensitivity to price change, not price differential, is usually regarded as a proper element to measure cross-elasticity of demand. [*American Crystal Sugar Co.* v. *Cuban-American Sugar Co.,* 259 F. 2d 524, 529-530 (2nd Cir. 1958)]

The question, which cannot be answered with precision or by a pat formula, is: How effective must be the competition in "the area of effective competition"? Evidentiary matters in addition to those stated above, include (1) degree of price sensitivity, (2) cross-elasticity of demand, (3) extent to which substitution occurs, (4) the manner in which the products are sold, and (5) the manner in which purchasers choose and buy. Statistical evidence can rarely, if ever, supply all the facts needed for a definitive judgment. [*U.S.* v. *Columbia Pictures Corp.,* 189 F. Supp. 153, 185 (S.D.N.Y. 1960)]

2. Importance of Barriers to Entry

Although there is no direct evidence in the record that beer is subject to high transportation costs, which would of course be highly persuasive evidence supporting the local-market theory, it is relevant that about 90% of beer sold in Wisconsin comes from breweries located in that State or nearby in Minnesota. To the extent that it is true that local breweries have an advantage in terms of efficiency and thus cost, a significant barrier exists to brewers who wish to sell in Wisconsin but brew their beer in other areas of the country. Thus, in terms of the structure of beer marketing as reflected in sales statistics and brewery location the record supports the relevancy of Wisconsin as a distinguishable and economically significant market for the sale of beer.

This picture of beer competition as essentially a localized or regional matter is buttressed by evidence of marketing techniques used by the industry. Beer is not a fungible commodity like wheat; product differentiation is important, and the ordinary consumer is likely to choose a particular brand rather than purchase any beer indiscriminately. The record demonstrates a recognition in the industry that a successful sales program relies to a large extent on consumer recognition and preference for particular brands, and that this preference must be built up through intensive advertising and other promotional techniques. [*U.S.* v. *Pabst Brewing Co.*, 384 U.S. 546, 559 (1966), Mr. Justice Harlan, concurring. (The status of an absence of barriers to entry as an affirmative defense is presently unclear—ed.)]

3. Interproduct Competition

Based on the evidence thus far revealed by this record we hold that the interindustry competition between glass and metal containers is sufficient to warrant treating as a relevant product market the combined glass and metal container industries and all end uses for which they compete. There may be some end uses for which glass and metal do not and could not compete, but complete interindustry competitive overlap need not be shown. We would not be true to the purpose of the Clayton Act's line of commerce concept as a framework within which to measure the effect of mergers on competition were we to hold that the existence of noncompetitive segments within a proposed market area precludes its being treated as a line of commerce. [*U.S.* v. *Continental Can Co.,* 378 U.S. 441, 457 (1964)]

It is quite true that glass and metal containers have different characteristics which may disqualify one or the other, at least in their present form, from this or that particular use; that the machinery necessary to pack in glass is different from that employed when cans are used; that a particular user of cans or glass may pack in only one or the other container and does not shift back and forth from day to day as price and other factors might make desirable; and that the competition between metal and glass containers is different from the competition between the can companies themselves or between the products of the different glass companies. These are relevant and important considerations but they are not sufficient to obscure the competitive relationships which this record so compellingly reveals. [*Ibid.,* 450]

III. AFFIRMATIVE DEFENSES

1. The Against Giants Defense

Congress, in enacting Clayton § 7, did not forbid all horizontal mergers but only those which may lessen competition substantially or tend to create a monopoly. Indeed, the legislative history of Clayton § 7 shows that Congress did not intend to impede mergers of smaller companies in order to enable them to compete more effectively with larger firms. [*U.S.* v. *Manufacturers Hanover Trust Co.,* 240 F. Supp. 867, 930 (S.D.N.Y. 1965)]

Appellant has presented no mitigating factors, such as . . . a demonstrated need for combination to enable small companies to enter into a more meaningful competition with those dominating the relevant markets. [*Brown Shoe Co.* v. *U.S.,* 370 U.S. 294, 346 (1962)]

. . . Defendant asserts that competition will be increased because Crystal and Colonial combined will be better able to compete with American, National, C&H and Great Western. Thus it is contended that a boost to a competitor of the pre-eminent firms in an industry is *pro tanto* a benefit to competition. Examination of this contention reveals that the term "competition" is therein used in two different, if not in fact adverse, ways. For, to the extent that a union of Crystal and Colonial would produce a stronger entity, it is true that the new firm would be a greater rival of other sugar refiners. It does not follow, however, that competition in the industry would thereby be increased. "Competition" is a descriptive term indicating the extent to which certain desirable types of market behavior occur. A union of two units of economic significance fails to give rise to a presumption that competition is thereby promoted; in the abstract such a union is inimical to independent pricing policies, price flexibility and the dispersion of market power. It is relevant to note that the legislative history of the 1950 Celler-Kefauver amendment to § 7 of the Clayton Act indicates that Congress conceived that substantial additions to concentration would be, in general, detrimental to competition. Certainly to the extent that a reduction in the number of significant firms in an industry reduces the incentive to reap a short term advantage by independent action, economic analysis indicates that increased concentration is detrimental to competition. In any event, that Colonial and Crystal when merged would form a stronger competitor does not by itself thereby establish that competition in the industry would be intensified. [*American Crystal Sugar Co.* v. *Cuban-American Sugar Co.*, 152 F. Supp. 387, 399-400 (S.D.N.Y. 1957)]

This merger cannot be defended on the ground that . . . the two had to merge to save themselves from destruction by some larger and more powerful competitor. This is not a "merger between two small companies to enable the combination to compete more effectively with larger corporations dominating the relevant market," . . . However, the Court today in a gratuitous dictum, *ante*, p. 277 undercuts even that principle by confining it to cases in which competitors are obliged to merge to save themselves from *destruction* by a larger and more powerful competitor. [*Ibid.*, 298, n. 28 (Mr. Justice Stewart, dissenting)]

2. The Failing Company Doctrine

. . . Supporters of the amendments indicated that it would not impede, for example, . . . a merger between a corporation which is financially healthy and a failing one which no longer can be a vital competitive factor in the market. [*Brown Shoe Co.* v. *U.S.*, 370 U.S. 294, 319 (1962)]

. . . It is doubtful that Cooke Trust would be able to earn sufficient profits from its trust business and the related business activities . . . to the extent that it would be economically feasible for it to continue in existence for a period in excess of a period of one to two years . . . if Cooke Trust were to continue in business in its present condition and without diminution in business or in staff, it would earn an estimated net profit of approximately $39,000, which sum would represent a return of about 1.5% on its value for liquidation purposes of approximately $2,500,000; . . . if Cooke Trust did continue in business it would probably suffer a diminution in both its business and its staff; that if the automatic stay in this case is not lifted, Cooke Trust will in all likelihood discontinue business and liquidate.

. . . No bank in Hawaii except the Bank proposed a merger with Cooke Trust; . . . it is doubtful if a merger with any other bank except Bank of Hawaii would have been feasible and Bank of Hawaii did not propose a merger; . . . it is doubtful if any of the smaller banks in Hawaii would have been able to absorb Cooke Trust as a unit and consequently would not have been able to adequately take care of the staff and clientele of Cooke Trust. [*U.S.* v. *First Nat. Bank of Hawaii*, 257 F. Supp. 591, 596 (D. Haw., 1966)]

Shopping Bag suffered from a lack of qualified executive personnel and, . . . although overall sales of the chain had been increasing, its earnings and profits were declining. Mr. Hayden, the president and principal stockholder of Shopping Bag, was advanced in years and was concerned over the absence of a strong management staff that could take over his responsibilities. [*U.S.* v. *Von's Grocery Co.*, 384 U.S. 270, 298 (1966), Mr. Justice Stewart, dissenting]

3. Natural Monopoly

In reality, Union Leader is attempting to relight the *ignis fatuus* over competition in a monopoly area. If Union Leader could enter and was not prevented from using its funds acquired in a monopoly market, supplemented, as it developed, by outside loans, we see no reason why its potential rivals should be subject to greater restrictions. Nor does the fact that an acquisition was involved automatically lead to a section 7 violation. If competition is doomed by market conditions, it cannot be "lessened" by a change of ownership. [*Union Leader Corp.* v. *Newspapers of New England, Inc.,* 284 F. 2d 582, 589 (1st Cir. 1960)]

4. Investment Exception

The defendants claim that the systems were purchased solely for investment and thus come within a specific exemption to § 7 of the Clayton Act. In support of this contention, they point out that in the fiscal year ending in February 1959, 62 per cent of Jerrold's total profit after taxes from all operations came from its operation of these acquired systems. While this evidence indicates that a major purpose of Jerrold in acquiring these systems was as an investment, it does not establish that this was a sole purpose. Jerrold obtained 100 per cent control of all these systems, except the one it later sold, and it owned 80 per cent of the latter. One would expect a wholly-owned subsidiary to purchase its equipment needs from its parent when the latter manufactures those items. Indeed, this is not a matter of pure speculation in this case, since the record discloses that Jerrold made sales to these subsidiaries from 1956 to 1959 totalling $426,338.85 and that no significant purchases were made from Jerrold's competitors during this period. Under the circumstances, the court cannot say that these acquisitions were made solely for investment. [*U.S.* v. *Jerrold Electronics Corp.,* 187 F. Supp. 545, 563 (W.D. Pa. 1960)]

PART III

Should Giant Corporations Be Dissolved?

A POLICY FOR ANTITRUST

Carl Kaysen and Donald F. Turner

Carl Kaysen is Director of the Institute for Advanced Study at Princeton, N.J., and the author of United States v. United Shoe Machinery Corporation: An Economic Analysis of an Antitrust Case *(Cambridge, Mass.: Harvard University Press, 1956). Donald F. Turner, on leave as Professor of Law at the Harvard Law School, is Assistant Attorney-General for Antitrust.*

. . . We suggest four alternative general goals for antitrust policy. They are (1) limitation of the power of big business; (2) performance (efficiency and progressiveness); (3) "fair dealing"; and (4) protection of competitive processes by limiting market power. . . . we select (4) as the most desirable and feasible guide, though willy-nilly and by design, the others will necessarily play some part.

A review of existing antitrust law indicates what to us are some important gaps in coverage. Since the existing law is primarily oriented toward conduct, it does not effectively deal—or at least has not effectively dealt in the past—with undue market power that cannot be associated with bad or unduly restrictive conduct. It seems clear that there now exist significant concentrations of undue market power, some individually held, some collectively "shared" in the sense that the members of the industry behave nonrivalrously for mutual benefit. . . . In addition, we believe that the law on

Carl Kaysen and Donald F. Turner, *Antitrust Policy: A Legal and Economic Analysis* (Cambridge, Mass.: Harvard University Press, 1959), pp. 44-48, 113-119, and 127-133. Copyright 1959 by the President and Fellows of Harvard College. Reprinted by permission of the authors and publisher.

conduct should be tightened in several respects if the prevention of undue market power is taken as a central guiding light.

In sum, we are suggesting that the primary goal of antitrust policy be the limitation of undue market power to the extent consistent with maintaining desirable levels of economic performance. . . . We propose amendments of the antitrust laws that would (1) enable a direct attack on undue market power without regard to the presence or absence of conspiracy in the legal sense, and (2) severely limit forms of conduct that contribute to, or are likely to contribute to, the creation of undue market power.

THE POLICY GOALS

Almost any policy proposal resolves itself into a statement of a hierarchy of ends, ordered to indicate which should prevail in situations where they conflict. In proposing that the primary goal of antitrust policy be the limitation of market power, we do not make it our sole goal; we also give great weight to the achievement of desirable economic performance. Indeed, in so far as reduction of market power is incompatible with efficiency and progressiveness, we subordinate the first goal to the second. If, for example, the efficient scale of operation in a particular market is so large in relation to the size of the market that efficient firms are so few in number as to make their possession of market power likely, and the reduction of market power cannot be achieved except at the cost of a substantial loss in efficiency, our policy would call for no action against the power itself. . . .

The other two of the broad classes of goals—promoting "fair" business conduct and the redistribution of social power between large and small business—occupy a much lower position in our hierarchy of policy aims. We expect that some degree of regulation of business conduct in the interest of "fair dealing" may be necessary. As we have already indicated, the policy of limiting market power will not be pressed to the point of reducing it to negligible dimensions everywhere (and indeed, this is not possible, even if it were viewed as desirable). Thus there may be some case for limiting the way in which residual market power is used. To the extent that some methods of using market power will be controlled on grounds that they are likely to contribute to the perpetuation of market power or to its increase, the area of regulation on pure "fair dealing" grounds will be correspondingly narrowed. But some kinds of conduct which will require such regulation do exist, and where it can be achieved without too high a price in efficiency, we deem it desirable. The following is a brief summary of our recommendations.

Limitation of Market Power

1. We propose statutory authorization for the reduction of undue market power, whether individually or jointly possessed; this to be done normally by dissolution, divorcement, or divestiture. We would except market power derived from economies of scale, valid patents, or the introduction of new processes, products, or marketing techniques.

2. We suggest, in the alternative, that the program be either (a) a permanent feature of antitrust policy, thus applying both to existing concentrations of market power and to concentrations that may later arise through inadequacies in the law, or in enforcement of the law, concerning conduct; or (b) a program limited to the time required to deal with existing undue concentrations of market power.

3. With respect to either of the above alternatives, we suggest that the policy might be carried out either (a) under a statute in which market power is defined in general terms, requiring a fairly extensive economic inquiry for determination of each case; or (b) under a statute in which market power is more arbitrarily defined, which would facilitate the disposition of cases and more clearly identify the "targets," but could possibly be applied to firms that, in fact, lacked market power.

Limitations on Conduct Contributing to Market Power

1. *Mergers*. Particularly if the proposals as to market power are deemed unwise or undesirable, and perhaps in any event, we propose tightening the law on mergers. . . . We propose, as one step in this direction, a requirement of advance reporting of all mergers involving firms of more than a certain absolute size in assets or more that a certain share of any market in which they operate. We also suggest the possibility of a more arbitrary standard for illegality, in line with the similar suggestion as to market power stated above.

2. *Price-fixing or price-influencing agreements.* Regarding trade association and similar collective activities, we propose specific statutory prohibition of agreements:

(a) to abide by reported list prices,

(b) to report offers at which no sales are made,

(c) to inform each other of the individual buyers and sellers in all transactions,

(d) to refuse to make reports, submitted to each other, available to buyers or buyers' trade associations,

(e) to submit books and accounts to the inspection of any member of the group or representative thereof; or

(f) to report transactions to each other, or to a representative of the group, within a period of seven days or less after said transactions take place.

3. *Collective refusals to deal.* Apart from those incidentally re-resulting from productive joint ventures, we would make collective refusals to deal illegal per se.

4. *Patents and patent licensing.* Proceeding on the basic premise that patentees' realizable rewards can be lowered without significantly reducing the flow of useful inventions and innovations, we propose:

(a) that the patent laws be revised to create a class of "petty" patents, with monopoly rights for five years only, and to raise the standard of invention for seventeen-year patents;

(b) that on restrictive clauses in patent licensing agreements,

(1) price-fixing clauses be made illegal per se,

(2) clauses providing for grant-backs of new patents or exclusive licenses thereunder be made illegal per se,

(3) covenants not to contest patent validity be invalid in any licensing agreement containing restrictions in addition to a uniform royalty provision,

(4) cross-licensing and pooling agreements contain no restrictions beyond that for a uniform royalty charge on each patent from all licensees (except that the owner may restrict the use), and

(5) all licensing agreements be registered with the Federal Trade Commission (but not made public);

(c) that Section 7 of the Clayton Act be revised to cover acquisitions of patents from individuals as well as from corporations.

5. *Price discrimination.* We propose that the Robinson-Patman

Act be repealed, in favor of a statute dealing separately with (a) price discrimination directed against competing sellers and (b) price discrimination that harms particular buyers. In each case, we would make some substantive changes in the existing law. In both cases, we would liberalize the "cost" defense and specifically exclude from the law all geographic price discrimination that is accounted for entirely by differences in transportation cost.

Procedural and Related Recommendations

1. We propose that criminal penalties be limited to the so-called per se offenses.

2. We propose that treble damages also be limited to the per se offenses; that no private suit be maintainable under a market power statutory provision; and that judgment under the market power provision would not constitute prima facie proof of anything under Section 5 of the Clayton Act.

3. We suggest the creation of a special court for adjudicating monopoly cases and other Sherman Act cases in which divestiture is part of the relief sought. For an extended program against undue market power, we propose a special court, with the prosecuting function placed in the hands of a new administrative agency. We also propose certain procedural steps designed to clarify and speed the trial of economic issues of fact. . . .

Remedies

The substantive effects of our proposed change in the law depend as much on what kinds of remedy orders the new law leads to as on the change in the standard of liability itself. The logic of our policy goal . . . calls for a widespread application of dissolution remedies, on the ground that an increase in numbers and reduction of concentration is the surest and most durable way of reducing market power. Thus, in most situations where the administrator of the law made a finding of unreasonable market power, the presumptive remedy would be the reduction in the size of the largest firms by divestiture and dissolution, within the limits of the rule against breaking up existing plants. There would be exceptions. First, our policy of not splitting up existing firms to the point of sacrificing demonstrable economies of scale would place limits on the amount of dissolution. It is worth noting that, typically, evidence relevant to the assertion of the reasonableness of existing market power would also be relevant to the determination of what these limits were. Second, there would be cases in which market power rested clearly on practices—say the existence of a closed patent pool, with territorial and product divisions. Here, if market concentration were not high, dissolution would appear unnecessary. Third, there may be cases in which the respondents could show that because of special circumstances, not relating to economies of scale, dissolution would result in a permanent loss of substantial economies. Fourth, it may be difficult to create new firms that would have a reasonable chance of survival. For example, one of the plants of a two-plant firm may be inefficient or badly located and thus incapable of effective competition as an independent unit.

Reorganization remedies, when applied, would not be limited to horizontal dissolution—splitting firms up into several smaller replicas with similar activities. In particular situations, vertical divestiture might be just as important or more important. Where market power rested on backward integration over scarce raw material resources or bottleneck transport facilities, this might be the case. Again, where distribution outlets were foreclosed by integration, vertical divestiture plus injunctions against achieving the effect of integration through exclusive dealing or other contractual devices might be indicated. In all these cases, a determination of liability which centered around defining the degree and sources of market power would produce the information on the basis of which appropriate remedy arrangements could be devised.

We base our presumption in favor of dissolution on the proposition that changing a tight oligopoly market into a looser one, or a market dominated by a single seller into one in which several large firms operate by reorganizing the larger firms in the market, will in fact change the market sufficiently so that the degree of market power exercised by the (still) relatively few large firms will be greatly reduced. Put crudely, the proposition is that the market with ten moderately large and thirty small firms will be much more competitive than the same one would be with four very large firms and thirty small ones. We also assume that the limits of reorganization we have suggested above will not be such as to prevent any effective program of increasing numbers from being put into effect.

Both experience—such as it is—and logic support the first proposition: the looser the oligopoly structure, the less market power any individual firm or the group as a whole exercises. Although evidence is scant, loose oligopoly industries such as oil refining and rayon appear to show more competitive behavior by the large firms than do tight ones such as cigarettes and flat glass. . . .

Further, the same reasons which make independent action rather than joint action more likely in a loose than in a tight oligopoly situation make it less likely that a well-functioning cartel can operate. In general, the larger the number of firms and the less important the relative position of the leading ones, the more is required in the way of machinery of information, communication, and enforcement to make an explicit agreement work. Given the illegality of such agreements, only those with a minimum of organized machinery can be expected to function undetected. Thus not only joint action based on "oligopolistic rationality," but also joint action based on an overt agreement, is less likely in practice the larger the numbers and the smaller the size of the leading firms in the market.

Finally, when the relative size (and thus the absolute size) of the largest sellers in a market is reduced, the entry barrier for new firms is, in general, also reduced. This arises from the fact that a significant element of the entry barrier is the superior liquid resources of existing firms in relation to most new ones; this puts the new entrant at a disadvantage in any "war" situation, price or otherwise, which existing sellers might initiate as a response to his entry. Given the fact that liquid funds are not freely available at the going price to the new entrant (or indeed, to any firm), the larger the absolute size of existing sellers, the greater is this disparity, and the greater this dimension of the risks associated with entry.

Our second assumption is that reorganization remedies can achieve significant changes in concentration within our stated limitations: no sacrifice of economies of scale or of substantial efficiencies unique to the firm, and the requirement that new firms created by divestiture have reasonable chance for survival. A well-buttressed conclusion on this point would require knowledge not now available, and unlikely to become available soon—unless as a by-product of our proposed policy. We simply cannot show in any detail, for example, what scale economies are available to the *firm* in the

relevant size range. But the available evidence . . . is consistent
with our assumption that they are not widespread.

Similarly, we doubt—to the point of perhaps striking it as a
defense—that there would be many cases where dissolution of a
firm would cause a permanent substantial loss of economies. We
reject completely the argument—sometimes implicit and sometimes
explicit in discussions of size and efficiency—that the only really
scarce resource is managerial talent. The argument is that large firms
exist because of the superior talents of their managers, and that any
obstacles placed in the way of their continued expansion will only
lead to the substitution of inferior for superior management, with
the consequent waste of resources. The argument has no support
in any evidence. . . .

The third limitation on reorganization remedies—that firms must
be created that have a reasonable chance of survival—may be of
considerable consequence. In this respect, the easily attained fea-
sibility of reorganizations under the Public Utility Holding Company Act, where each new independent company was a "natural
monopoly," can give little comfort. We would suppose it to be the
rule rather than the exception that there will be at least some variations in efficiency among the plants of a multiplant firm, and, in the
case of a firm producing many products, varying degrees of specialization among plants that may have at least some bearing on their
respective fates as independent firms.

Injunctive Remedies

Even if reorganization remedies become typical in market power
cases, as here proposed, injunctive remedies directed toward conduct will still occupy an important place in the administration of
the law in cases in which market power is the primary issue. First
of all, the limits to reorganization remedies will be of sufficient importance in some cases so that there may still be reason to control
the conduct of the respondent firms. Such control will be directed
toward two goals: the abolition of practices which contributed to
the maintenance of market power by the respondents, and secondarily, to proscribing unfair or exploitative conduct. The first aim
may also be important even when there has been a dissolution
remedy; some restraint for a period of years on the practices of

the successor firms may be necessary to get the full benefits of dissolution in the reduction of market power. For example, in a situation in which patents had played an important role in buttressing the power of a large firm, a remedy might include both dissolution and an injunction directed to the successor firms forbidding exclusive cross-licensing of patents among them. Secondly, there will always be situations in which structural remedies are impossible. . . .

Administrative Feasibility

How feasible are our proposals for market power liability and for widespread use of reorganization remedies? It may be that they strain the capacities of an administrative system dependent on the attorney general and the courts, and that any serious effort to put them into practice would require a different procedure for producing remedy orders than that now operating. But some general comments can be offered here without discussing the problem of suitable administrative machinery, which we take up in a later chapter. The change in the standard of liability would effect an important change in the kind of information produced in and by the enforcement process. Respondent firms, in attempting to show that their market power was reasonable, would necessarily assemble and discuss most of the information relevant to a judgment on how much dissolution was feasible, if any. To be sure, important problems of evaluation on which respondents' judgments would differ from those offered by the government would remain. In general, respondents' judgments on such matters would be based on closer knowledge and greater *expertise* than those offered by the other side, though they could hardly claim to be disinterested. But even this problem is not insuperable. Once respondents knew that they were bound to suffer some amount of reorganization, they would have a substantial interest in presenting some feasible plan, although not perhaps the most drastic feasible plan. As representatives of their stockholders, the managements of respondent firms would be concerned to see that any reorganization proposals put into effect did in fact create viable successor firms, so that their stockholders were not disadvantaged unnecessarily. This interest, plus the criticism by the other side inherent in the adversary proceedings, would prevent the offer of impractical plans or the failure to offer any at all on the part of respondents. For this process to work, however, a minimum condition is that the level of knowledge in the relevant areas of economics and industrial engineering available to the government in such proceedings be far higher than it is now in the typical presentation of an antitrust case. . . .

MERGERS

Nature of the Problem

. . . The history of merger movements shows clearly that mergers have been one of the major routes by which large firms achieved dominant positions in their markets. It is clear that some policy which prevents or limits mergers is of central importance in a pro-competitive program. To be sure, we could wait for mergers to occur and deal with their consequences, when necessary, along the lines already suggested, but the wastefulness of a procedure which first allows merger and then, after a lengthy and costly proceeding, severs what has been joined, hardly needs laboring.

The problem lies rather in the other direction. If mergers have been the royal road to monopoly and oligopoly in the past, why not simply forbid them altogether? We must begin, therefore, by considering the important reasons for mergers other than the achievement of dominant size and the elimination of competition. From the standpoint of ownership and management in the small or moderate-sized firm which is frequently the acquired firm in a merger, several important motives for selling can be discerned. First, there is often a lack of management succession when present executives reach retirement age, or die without trained successors. Second, a retiring owner-manager may prefer a more diversified investment portfolio than that represented by his own business; this may be especially important in respect to building an estate. Third, there is the difference between the capital-gains tax and the income tax, which may stimulate the retention of earnings rather than their withdrawal as dividends, and the subsequent sale of the business so built-up for the capital gain. All these reasons make the maintenance of some market for going businesses an important part of the incentives to the owner-manager to build up and run a business. Forbidding all mergers would reduce significantly the rewards of the entrepreneur in just the area where individual entrepreneurship is still important. . . .

From the standpoint of both buyers and sellers, mergers may promote efficiency. Where the appropriate scale of operations or degree of integration of the firm changes, mergers may provide the most economical method of reshaping the structures of existing firms to the new cost conditions. Similarly, where a particular line of activity is declining, the acquisition of firms engaged in it by firms in expanding markets may be the most economical way to salvage the assets of the declining firms, providing a much greater social as well as private transfer-value than could be achieved if the organization were destroyed and the capital assets sold in the second-hand market.

The special circumstances which stimulate mergers in order to acquire quotas, licenses, and transferable tax offsets may be ignored as inappropriate to determining policy because they simply involve transfers of income rather than changes in real costs or outputs and because some of them are undesirable in themselves— e.g., the tax incentives to acquiring deficit firms. The desirability of the kind of arbitraging which takes place in the capital market when divergences between stock prices and replacement values of assets stimulate mergers may be assigned a relatively low weight as a factor in policy. But the other reasons for mergers cannot be similarly dismissed in formulating antitrust policy with respect to mergers.

Our problem then is to gain the advantages of prohibiting mergers which serve to increase market power, yet to do so with as little effect as possible on the market for business assets, or on the availability of the merger as a method of entry in markets that are new for the merging firm, or on the possibilities of increasing efficiency through mergers.

The Present Law

. . . The primary issue is the kind of proof that will be deemed sufficient to establish the probability of a "substantial lessening of competition" or a "tendency to monopoly." In this respect the legislative history of the 1950 amendment is not particularly enlightening, to say the least. It was clearly intended that less need be shown in a Section 7 proceeding than would be required to strike down a merger under the Sherman Act. At the same time, the committee reports accepted the proposition, set forth in the *International Shoe* case, that a probability of substantial harm, not a mere possibility, must be shown. It is difficult to reconcile these two positions, since an informal judgment as to future probabilities would seem to demand an inquiry of as broad a range, if not as penetrating a depth, as is required in establishing past effects.

One way out of this corner is to decide that the requisite probability of harm shall be conclusively presumed on the basis of certain specified showings. *Standard Stations,* a Section 3 case, is the classic example of this approach, holding that exclusive-requirements contracts are illegal whenever they foreclose "a substantial share of the line of commerce affected." Whether such an approach may be called a compromise of the two positions taken in the legislative reports, or is instead an abandonment of any serious effort to determine actual probabilities, depends on whether the selected conclusive presumption makes sense for the generality of cases. Be that as it may with regard to Section 3—is a "quantitative share" test, or variant thereof, to be applied here?

DuPont-GM clearly says that it is in so far as vertical acquisitions are concerned. "Foreclosures" of a substantial share of the "relevant market" by vertical acquisition will receive the same treatment as foreclosure by exclusive contracts. Moreover, unless *DuPont-GM* is *sui generis* because of the large size of the companies involved, the "relevant market" will be narrowly defined; no *Cellophane* refinements will be pertinent in a Section 7 vertical merger proceeding.

It is not certain, however, that the Court would similarly dispose of horizontal mergers. There is an argument that the two kinds of mergers are distinguishable. For one thing, a "foreclosure" test is literally inapplicable to horizontal mergers; per se, such a merger forecloses neither competing sellers from access to buyers, nor buyers from access to those sellers. The direct quantitative impact of a vertical merger is missing. It may be reasonable to decide that a conclusive presumption of probable harm shall apply to a merger of two competitors who are both "quantitatively substantial" in their market, or to any more than *de minimis* acquisition by an already powerful firm, but the justification is much more involved than that supporting the apparent rule on vertical mergers. . . .

No light whatever can be shed on the probable status of "conglomerate" mergers, which the committee reports on the 1950 amendment indicated were to be covered by revised Section 7. We are inclined to believe that few if any true conglomerate merger cases—entirely devoid of both vertical and horizontal aspects—will be brought, if for no other reason than that standards of illegality seem wholly elusive. Most mergers that crudely appear to be conglomerate will prove to have vertical or horizontal elements or both if the markets involved are carefully analyzed and defined. The Hazel Atlas, Continental Can merger, for example, is "conglomerate" only on the assumption that cans and bottles are completely noncompetitive.

How Should the Law Be Interpreted?

The key question in any interpretation of Section 7 is, What meaning shall be given to the characterizing phrase "the effect of such acquisition may be substantially to lessen competition, or tend to create a monopoly"? It is this phrase which defines the mergers Section 7 forbids.

In order to carry out the logic of our policy goal—the limitation of market power—we would propose initially that any merger which appears likely to create market power (as we have defined it) where none existed before, or to increase pre-existing market power, should be banned by the law. Since the test applies to market power which will or will not be present in a future situation, it must necessarily be couched in terms of probabilities. What is outlawed are mergers which have a substantial probability of creating the undesirable effects, not those which conceivably might do so. For purely horizontal mergers, or for what might be called the horizontal elements in a merger—involving firms which compete in the same market—both the creation and enhancement of market power must be considered. For vertical mergers, or vertical elements in a merger, only the enhancement or extension of market power is relevant, since a nonhorizontal merger cannot create such power where it did not exist before. But it can, through the leverage effects of firms in one market on those in another to which they stand in the relation of supplier or customer, enhance existing power, or enable it to be applied in a new market.

If our general test were to be taken strictly, the government would in general be required to offer proof similar to that which would be relevant in a market power proceeding. . . . In a horizontal merger case, the government would have to show either that the acquiring firm already has market power, which the acquisition would detectably enhance, or that market power would probably result from the merger. In a vertical merger case, the government would need to show existing market power, plus a probability that it would be extended into the new field or enhanced by the acquisition (such as the acquisition of a source of raw material that is in short supply). But in so far as the proof concerns future probabilities rather than presenting existing facts, it would differ in some respects from that appropriate to a market power proceeding. In particular, much more reliance would have to be placed on structural evidence, since behavioral evidence would normally be available only for the market as it has existed in the past. At best, therefore, a strict application of the market power approach to mergers would involve some resort to presumptions if the antimerger program were to be at all feasible administratively. . . .

To be somewhat more specific, we would establish the following propositions as bench marks:

1. *Vertical mergers.* An acquisition of a relatively substantial customer or supplier by a firm with 20 percent of its primary market is prima facie illegal.

2. *Horizontal mergers.* (a) Any acquisition of a competitor by a firm with 20 percent or more of its market is prima facie illegal. (b) Any merger of competitors who together constitute 20 percent or more of a market is prima facie illegal.

3. A merger prima facie illegal can be justified only by convincing proof that (a) the acquired company is in failing or obviously declining circumstances, or (b) the acquisition will yield substantial economies of scale or economies in resource utilization that cannot be effected feasibly in any other way (e.g., internal expansion or the acquisition of assets from other than a competitor, customer, or supplier).

The criteria of prima facie illegality would not, of course, preclude the government from establishing probable ill effects from mergers involving firms of smaller relative size. Severe limitations on entry, the fact that the acquired company has been an active influence on prices—these and other factors would warrant a finding of illegality on the basis of fairly small market shares. . . .

THE ECONOMIC IMPACT OF ANTITRUST: AN OVERVIEW

Simon N. Whitney

Simon N. Whitney is Professor of Economics at New York University. He is the author of Antitrust Polices (New York: The Twentieth Century Fund, 1958).

A. VIEWS OF ECONOMISTS SUMMARIZED

The nearly universal support for the principle of antitrust among academic economists is not surprising, trained as all are in the principles of a competitive market economy. It is not surprising either that they disagree (compare their clashes on fiscal and monetary policies) on aspects of its practical application. . . .

The major agreement in economists' current views can be put into this nutshell: the antitrust laws have contributed (1) substantially, to prevent the cartelization of the economy; but (2) only in certain industries (e.g., petroleum refining, tobacco, explosives, motion pictures), to reduce existing concentration. The disagreement is in whether this failure calls for new policies. . . . Most economists writing on antitrust appear to favor a campaign against oligopoly. . . . Court decisions . . . have established Section 7 as a strong obstacle to *increased* concentration (except as this takes the form of size through diversification). Most economists also believe that competition is now fairer than before 1914—i.e., that unethical, oppressive or predatory practices in business have been reduced. . . .

The Antitrust Bulletin, IX (1964), 510-543. Copyright 1964, Federal Legal Publications.

Moving on now to the more interesting issue of disagreement, I shall approach it . . . through . . . [two] books dealing with antitrust:

Joe S. Bain, *Industrial Organization,* John Wiley (1959). . . .

Carl Kaysen and Donald F. Turner, *Antitrust Policy,* Harvard University Press (1959). . . .

The viewpoints on our critical issue may be summarized as follows: . . . Kaysen and Turner's book is essentially a brief for a program of corporate dissolution, and Bain's textbook endorses their program. . . . The rest of this article will expand [the] minority position . . . through comments on the proposal of Kaysen and Turner. Their book, packed with able analysis, and characterized in a foundation-sponsored, private circulated, report on antitrust research as the most valuable work done in the last fifteen years, evidently deserves attention. This will not be a balanced . . . review, however; nor will it cover their other proposals. It will concentrate on the dissolution plan as the most detailed presentation to date of a policy favored by many economists.

B. A PROPOSED DISSOLUTION FORMULA

A campaign of "dissolution, divorcement, divestiture" (Walter Adams, 27 *Indiana L. J.* 1) has been urged over the years by many, including the 1964 president of the American Economic Association (George J. Stigler). Thus the Twentieth Century Fund Committee on Cartels and Monopoly (three members out of six had taught economics) called in 1951 for:

. . . a rebuttable presumption against the retention by any enterprise of a position that enables it to control more than a fixed percentage of the market for any product or related group of products.

Kaysen and Turner have brought the issue nearer the point where it can be sensibly debated, with their draft statute (pp. 266-72) and list of target industries (pp. 275-80). The relevant parts of the statute, which provides for an Industrial Reorganization Commission to prosecute cases before a panel of judges specializing in this work on eight-year assignments, are excerpted herewith:

. . . market power shall mean the persistent ability of a person, or of a group . . . to restrict output or determine prices without losing a substantial share of the market, or without losing substantial profits . . . Evidence . . . may include . . . (1) persistent failure of prices to reflect substantial declines of demand or costs, or . . . substantial excess capacity; (2) persistence of profits that are abnormally high, taking into account such factors as risks and excess capacity; or (3) failure of new rivals to enter the market during prolonged periods of abnormally high profits . . .

. . . Market power shall be deemed unreasonable unless shown by defendant . . . to have been created and maintained, entirely or almost entirely, by . . . (1) such economies as are dependent upon size . . . (2) . . . valid patents . . . (3) low prices or superior products attributable to . . . new processes, product improvements or . . . efficiency . . . in comparison with . . . other firms having a substantial share of the market.

The Economic Court . . . shall . . . order . . . divestiture . . . provided that: (1) the court shall not approve . . . division of the assets of a single plant; (2) . . . shall take into account any probable permanent loss of substantial economies . . . (3) . . . shall not order division . . . where . . . such relief would not materially improve the competitive conditions . . . (4) . . . or . . . companies resulting from the plan would lack reasonable prospects for survival . . .

The "probable area of application" of the program would be the 57 industries, out of 147 with national markets, in which 8 firms account for 50 percent of shipments—or perhaps only the 41 in which they account for 75 percent (p. 94, footnote). Five more concentrated industries are found to have "regional" markets (petroleum refining is the largest), but are not named as early dissolution targets. Only one set of percentages is made part of the draft statute: that market power shall be conclusively presumed where for five years one company has made 50 percent of sales or four companies 80 percent.

My review will begin with the three criteria of unreasonable market power and the authorized defenses, then proceed to the potential results of the policy, and end with its original justification. In each area, I shall raise objections whose purpose is to push the debate on this "hottest" issue in antitrust economics nearer to acceptable conclusions.

C. PROPOSED CRITERIA OF UNREASONABLE MARKET POWER AND POSSIBLE REBUTTALS

1. Prices Not Declining with Demand, Costs, or Capacity Utilization

Declines in demand may affect general business, one industry, or one company. A price reduction would often, or usually, help revive sales—but a court, even an "economic" court, presumably decides each case on its own individual facts. Should failure to cut prices be a criterion when price reduction is not called for in the particular market situation?

Two serious difficulties in trying to stem a general decline in demand by a general price reduction are the resistance of so many prices to downward pressures and the danger of a spiral once a decline begins. National policy long ago switched to public spending as a preferred remedy (Kaysen and Turner, p. 197). The best known examples of prices held firm despite declining demand have occurred, however, in such periods of general recession—e.g., published prices, and to a large extent transaction prices, of some metals and durable goods (along with union wage rates, freight rates, property tax rates, and the like) in years like 1930 and 1958. The quick revivals of demand in 1949, 1954, 1958, and 1961 would have allowed little time for due process of law to be applied to most industries accused of tardy price cutting.

Changing the assumption to one of reduced demand in a single industry, let us phrase antitrust charges fitted to two actual and two hypothetical situations in industries on the target list:

"Passenger car sales have fallen; yet you failed to cut prices, using the ancient arguments that this is merely an offyear, that customers who have already bought will be resentful, and that you will have to apply the cut to dealer floor stocks. We can neither wait to check your forecast of recovery nor take account of guesses as to buyers' opinions." "Jet planes are replacing propeller planes;

you switched to other products instead of reducing propeller prices to persuade the airlines to abandon the jet idea."

Hypothetically: "The American public is using less sugar. You point to declining output and rising use abroad which are raising world prices, but we are enforcing a law to protect the American consumer." "Cigarette sales have fallen due to health worries; you should have cut prices to induce people to smoke as much as before despite their fears."

When demand is shifting between industries, a legal investigation will be another blow to the one which is losing out, absorbing the efforts of its executives and damaging its self-confidence and public "image." More important, would an industry charged with price maintenance when demand declined be allowed to plead failure of costs to decline? Some costs have a rather rigid character. Would a plea of low cash reserves, which might run out if the price cut did not quickly restore the former volume—plus enough additional to offset the lower prices—be acceptable? Should the court, even with its average four-year experience in economic matters, second-guess managements on elasticity of demand or on probable costs?

Prices are established by individual companies rather than industries. When Packard cut prices in response to declining demand, it lost its quality reputation. Would a sophisticated economic court ignore product quality and the consumer image a given defendant had been seeking for its product? If Kent or Camel advertising drew customers away from Pall Mall, could the latter escape a charge of price maintenance only by becoming an "economy cigarette"?

Can equity within an industry be preserved? If the dominant firm has maintained its sales, but its smaller (though still oligopolistic) competitors have not, should it be blamed if they fail to cut prices? Conversely, if it ought to have cut prices but did not, are the smaller firms also to be penalized for not starting a price war from which they might have feared bankruptcy? In general, will all the large corporations in an industry be subject to attack, or only the "unreasonable" ones?

If costs decline, we would expect prices to be cut, but by how much? When the reduction in costs results from management initiative, a compensating price cut could remove the incentive for further efforts. Yet cost reductions not resulting from cheaper raw materials normally originate with management rather than in offers of employees or tax collectors to take less. Or, if machinery producers offer a new product which adds to efficiency of their customers, the latter must at least make the decision to buy the machinery. What returns on the capital investment which financed cost reductions will the court allow? Can involvement in regulating rates of return by some such back door be escaped?

Giving this special weight to price cutting might mean slighting product improvement, with its decisive role in our rising standard of living. More and better stockings did not come from price competition in cotton, but from a monopolist's introduction of nylon. Fortunately, the draft statute appears to leave companies the right to use cost savings in product improvement. This should reduce the number of defendants—e.g., Chevrolet's improvement of product, which suited consumers better than Ford's continued price cutting in the early 1920's, would not have been condemned.

If unused capacity is charged, how will the judges assess something which has escaped any generally acceptable measurement by statisticians, economists and business men to date? Might the supposed excess capacity be obsolete? Would Bethlehem Steel build a new Indiana mill if it added to capacity statistics and might draw a divestiture suit? Is it wise to put pressure on companies to shut down stand-by facilities?

2. Persistence of High Profits in Relation to Risk and Capacity

Abnormal profits, allowing for risks and excess capacity, are to be a second evidence of market power. Apparently a company should never make more than normal profits, unless its risk factor is unusually high; but if it has idle capacity, it should make less than normal profits. Over a cycle, this averages out to something below normal. Charts which correlate profits with utilized capacity (usually for U.S. Steel) are informative—though they might be coupled with correlations of steel wages and employment—but are they good enough to be legal evidence?

Economists have not yet put the relations of risk and profits into figures. Some who argue that the risks do not justify the profits would be unwilling to take the risks themselves. To illustrate a major difficulty, let us assume an industry in which 20 firms have participated, of which 10 have failed or sold out to avoid failure. Profits are abnormal by standards of other industries, but are they high in relation to the risk which the 10 companies went through to attain their present "security"? If such past risks cannot be counted, companies entering an industry would have to consider (1) risks of failure, (2) hopes of abnormal profits as long as some competitors were obviously failing, and (3) thereafter, a return to more normal profits. If this prospect reduced the desire to enter, a consequence would be lower output, and more profits for those already in.

Risk and market power cannot explain the greater profitability of some firms than of others in the same industry. The risks are common to all, they compete in one market, but profits differ. Evidently management success differs. Perhaps the vital decisions which set the companies on their courses were made in the past. Some are probably still being made, with success being achieved in continuing innovations, skill in pleasing the public, and operating efficiency. Some well known corporations, and others less known, have thus earned persisting high profits in relation to risk and capacity—and to competitors.

Kaysen and Turner offer a rebuttal: no such continuing success of a firm in competition is possible, since better managers of one company will be hired away by others, and better methods copied (pp. 9-10). Members of "theatre companies" may stay put, out of loyalty, but not executives of a commercial organization. Nevertheless, despite the "article of democratic faith" that there are enough equally good managers for a few hundred companies, some do keep ahead. If individual managers retire or leave, it appears that the management *system* stays. After a long enough period—a few decades in the case of the first Henry Ford, though it might take much longer when a system rather than a man is in question—the secret of profit-making may be lost. We cannot speak surely of indefensible profit persistence over any such period as five, ten, or even twenty years.

Less successful companies do copy management methods proved superior—perhaps after several years. Will the new antitrust mechanism allow time for them to succeed and to achieve equal profits, before it proceeds against the originator of the superior methods (and thus perhaps raises its costs to equal those of the rest)? Alternatively, if it proceeds only against whole industries, must the less profitable competitors be punished for the "fault" of the more profitable ones?

Although they see "no evidence" that "superior management" is a frequent factor in lower costs (p. 117), the authors do leave in their statute possible defenses based on economies of size, and on low prices or superior products due to a firm's efficiency. But efficiency expressing itself in profits or in market expansion is not recognized. The book's concept of efficiency also rejects superior ability to please consumers. . . .

3. Failure of New Firms to Enter a Profitable Industry

If new firms dare not enter, should existing ones be blamed? Can we punish A, which did have the courage to enter, for B's lack of courage?

Reasons for non-entry into profitable large-scale industries include, among others: (1) realization that adding one more firm to those now operating in a market will reduce profits to a level that the new one, at least, would find unsatisfactory; (2) lack of any prospect of matching the efficient working organizations, distribution arrangements, and product popularity of established companies; and (3) if room in the market and efficiency of the would-be entrant are present, fear that established firms will attack it with discriminatory price cutting in its own particular product or geographic market.

That the source of these three fears is not necessarily "unreasonable" market power may be seen by looking at them in the light of the divestiture proposal. Where the first reason prevails, dissolution would not attract entry. Where the second prevails, dissolution would appear in the unattractive guise of a method of raising costs of existing companies to the point where inexperienced newcomers could match them. The terrors of reason (3) would be mitigated by breaking up existing firms, but the *American Tobacco* and *United Shoe Machinery* decisions have already held that price reductions by dominant firms designed to oust new competitors are evidence of monopolizing.

One aspect of reason (2) is often put in a separate category—i.e., product popularity is assumed to have its origin in massive advertising rather than any meritorious conduct of the existing company. This is only in part true. Intelligence in discovering what consumers will buy, and in maintaining as well as boasting about quality of product, are necessary to attract and hold enough customers. Many of us do buy inferior products at higher prices because of advertising, but human gullibility (the glib traveling salesman is said to have made the sale in earlier days) will not be removed by dissolution. From the tobacco divestitures of 1911 grew the modern advertising boom. Plymouth and Chevrolet, even after they are independent companies, will still display their merits in the same media as now.

The automobile industry is an extreme example of nonentry: few others can be as vulnerable on this count. The less chance there is of a newcomer matching the costs or public appeal of the existing companies—i.e., the better adapted existing companies are to supply the wants of the public—the less tenable the legal situation of the industry becomes.

Most major industries have had occasional entries. One wonders what time limit the court will allow before it decides entry has been inadequate. Once the new firms have come in, must they stay in as well, to take the curse off existing firms?

4. Permissible Rebuttals to Charges of Unreasonable Market Power

Defendants are assigned the burden of proof to show that their market power was "created and maintained, entirely or almost entirely," by economies of size, by valid patents, or by low prices or superior products resulting from innovation or efficiency. The quoted clause is a strong one. It would be a rare case in which the prosecution could not produce at least *some* additional cause of the market power, at least on some past occasion, besides the three which are permitted. Even in industries renowned for efficiency among management experts (e.g., automobiles, some chemicals, business equipment), there have been mergers, tying contracts and other actions often leading to antitrust suits. These might be unimportant in the industry's present success and yet be enough to rebut any claim of past success "entirely or almost entirely" due to efficiency.

The draft statute, in setting up these possible defenses, excludes such possibilities as a firm having lower costs and using its savings gradually to expand its position in the market, or selling increasing quantities simply because buyers prefer its products whether a court might consider them "superior" or not.

No divestiture shall involve "any probable permanent loss of substantial economies." "Any" and "probable" should work in favor of defendants, but "substantial" may not. Will the judges think the usual loss of personnel, financial, purchasing, and selling economies "substantial"? "Permanent" is still less likely to be interpreted in defendants' favor, as this would require a court to speculate on possibilities in the infinite future.

The authors themselves do not expect any of these clauses to help many defendants—e.g., "scale economies . . . to the *firm* in the relevant size range . . . are not widespread" (p. 116); "the patent office is applying far too loose a standard of patentability" (p. 171); neither the patent defense nor that of "superior products" is likely to be "quantitatively important" (p. 79); and the "probable permanent loss" will be used so little that it should perhaps be omitted altogether (p. 116).

D. PRACTICAL PROBLEMS IN DISSOLVING FIRMS WITH MARKET POWER

The authors evidently consider the difficulties in applying their proposal to be "serious" (p. 59), though less so than those in any alternative proposal. Different problems, for the most part, occurred to them and to me. I make no claim that all those I mention will be important or that none can be solved. I simply did not find solutions in the book.

1. Can the proposal be equitably applied? For example, can the criteria of timing and magnitude of such offenses as fixed prices and high profits be made exact enough so that potential defendants can try to live within the law? Can an offending firm, but never its competitor, be sued? Are we prepared to say that the property

rights of owners of companies which have, in reliance on the law as it stood to date, expanded and built additional plants—sometimes at the urging of the Federal or State governments—should be sacrificed because we are certain the new policy will benefit the nation?

2. Might the plan reward caution or trickery? Could industries escape by varying their prices artificially, or helping new but weak firms to enter their fields? Will growing companies expand single plants beyond the optimum point rather than become vulnerable by building additional plants? Would General Motors shut down for a while each fifth year in those lines (e.g., locomotives or buses) where its share was running largest? Can the commission's analysis and the court's decisions, in general, keep up with changing technology and markets?

3. The great majority of potential defendants are diversified. Companies will often be big in some product markets, small in others. Some which own several plants concentrate a particular product in one, making these exempt. Some plants make several products, of which one or a few, but not all, might be in concentrated industries. Many industries are complexes of interrelationships whose efficiency could suffer from the rough justice of divestiture. I have not canvassed the possibilities, but neither, it appears, have the authors.

4. The authors grant that where one plant is less efficient or less well located than others it might not survive competitively (p. 114). This important admission should be widened by noting that among the typical reasons for building additional plants has been the desire to obtain more modern facilities or a plant closer to some important market. Even if two plants are equally modern, their competition will be minimized if each is closer to its own market.

5. Details aside, is there not a potential conflict between the whole policy and the principles on which our economy has hitherto operated? Business firms have always been encouraged to grow. Would they have responded had it been known that legal action might follow? Should we take the motivation of any economic group, such as investors or managers, for granted, when we pass new rules? If we want economic growth, should we by adopting this plan warn those who are thinking of building that "excess capacity" may mean an antitrust suit?

Here is a difficulty which the authors have recognized. Their first answer is that firms will still be free to grow without mergers, provided they do not become "large relative to any market" (p. 86). This is a stiff proviso. Would an expanding company—say, one whose research has given it a chance to launch a new fiber, plastic, or drug which might sweep its market—have faith that the federal commission and court (some members perhaps chosen partly for their antitrust zeal) would interpret each supporting action as normal growth? The authors go on to say that, if the entrepreneurial spirit survived the New Deal policies—labor, financial, tax, and holding company—it can surely survive their own "modest" suggestion. They think it "unlikely" that the crackdown on some firms will hurt the entrepreneurial spirit elsewhere, and they may well be right. Whenever Congress is in a venturesome mood, it could make the experiment.

6. To which industries will the policy be applied? Let us use the first sub-table, covering the eight largest concentrated industries with national markets and "geographically concentrated supply," as our example.

The first industry named is aircraft engines and propellers. Until the new policy is cleared with the Department of Defense and the Federal aviation authorities, I think we can forget its application here.

Number two is cigarettes. It is well known that after the 1946 *American Tobacco* case divestiture proposals were blocked by the impossibility of dividing the ownership of popular brands. The "big three" cigarettes, which accounted for 78 percent of sales in 1946 (and seemed to the Supreme Court in so strong a position), accounted for only a third as large a share in 1962. Inability to divide trademarks is less of a problem now, due to the rise of new brands as a result of the health question and of active competition (under oligopoly). But, if Camel, Winston, and Salem could be separated now (I believe they share some joint facilities at Winston-Salem), two might easily in a few years be selling 50 percent more than today, with the other no longer seriously competing.

In plastics materials, it is common for one research department to serve all the plants of a producer. The competitive survival of a successor plant forced to build its research from scratch, without economies of scale, must be doubtful. Another problem, though less serious, will arise in disposing of, and later managing, the one raw material plant which sometimes supplies several plants making plastics and resins.

Synthetic fibers is number four. Waiving the research difficulty, du Pont, at least, could be dissolved, since it has several plants. Imprudently, it would then appear, it attempted to keep pace with the public demand for the fibers it had developed.

In copper rolling and drawing, one could separate eastern and western plants. Due to the distance factor, the additional competition might not be very great.

Number six is tractors. International Harvester makes wheel tractors in a single plant. With the largest farm equipment producer exempt, no doubt the small ones would be left alone. In crawler tractors, Caterpillar Tractor could probably set its small plant free to compete against its retained big plant.

In motor vehicles and parts, one wonders about the remedy. An assembly plant in California will hardly seek the same customers as plants in New Jersey and Georgia. If Cadillac and Chevrolet are divorced, the typical buyer will scarcely be choosing between them. Even the Buick-Oldsmobile-Pontiac competition will merely increase a rivalry that already exists among them. What will be the survival prospects of a company making only one line of cars, and selling in one consumer market, if it meets two or three bad years in a row? Reorganizing parts supply would also surely be a task of the greatest complexity.

The eighth and last industry in this group is wine and distilled liquors. Three of the four dominant companies are Canadian. Whoever inherits the Seagram name will for the present be the largest seller.

Some of the industries in which four companies for five years have accounted for 80 percent of sales are: aluminum, cereal breakfast foods, chewing gum, computers, copper, etc. This may give a conclusive presumption of unreasonableness, but the array of difficulties remains. If we want copper prices reduced to a more competitive level, we can cut the tariff or redivide mine ownership. Pressure on wages, and unemployment, will soon cause us to hear from the copper miners. If the authorities go through the IBM organization deftly and break its research, production, and distribution sections into parts, and if they stay as they are put, it will

probably be because progress has stopped. Perhaps we can break
the chewing gum trademarks and get prices below five cents and
consumption increased!

To summarize: many or most industries seem likely to win exemption through the single-plant clause, the efficiency defense (if
allowed to firms like du Pont and IBM), the rules that relief must
improve competition and not imperil survival, international com-
plications, and trademarks. If the reply of proponents is that establishing the principle will cause the details to fall into place, or that
it is these difficulties which the new government commission and
courts will be paid to solve, we shall just have to wait and see what
happens.

E. THE JUSTIFICATION
FOR A DIVESTITURE PROGRAM

Difficulties as great as the foregoing suggest that the supporters
of this policy might rethink their ground. Does our economy, then,
operate so badly that we must take these chances? . . .

Critics will certainly not deny that the economy, whatever its
faults, has on the whole succeeded in its function of producing
goods for a growing population, with expanding private and public
demands, and without as yet destroying our democratic institutions.
This being accepted, two possible defenses of any drastic program
remain: "So far, so good—but I can demonstrate theoretically that
my plan will improve the results without risking what we have
now," and "So far, so good—but the trend of concentration means
these good results will not continue." The first argument would call
for considerable confidence in one's theory, the second for convincing statistical evidence.

Our industrial system has serious faults, some of them curable
and others inseparable from its virtues. There are big firms that
make less effective use of their resources than small ones; others
do well at times and poorly at other times. If we could draw on
experts omniscient in industry and economics, they could do better
than the market in moving firms toward the right sizes and the
right policies. The question is whether the proposed legal machinery
can do it.

1. Kaysen and Turner's Argument

The single sentence most clearly offered in justification of the proposal is probably the following:

It is the fact that the competitive market *compels* the results of its processes which is the ultimate defense against the demand that economic decisions be made or supervised by politically responsible authorities. (p. 48)

In other words, if our economic benefits do not flow from "market compulsions," the people will insist some day on government ownership or much more detailed regulation. No evidence for this political forecast is given, and little is obvious on the political scene.

This belief that industry decisions should be dictated by the market rather than planned in the board room or office is held by some other economists as well. It has been said that when management has produced better goods in quantity at acceptable prices, it was because they "happened for the moment to be benevolent or 'smart.'" Benevolence is hard to see as a major motive. Smartness may be granted, in the sense of recognizing the money to be made in foreseeing what consumers will want and supplying it at prices they can afford to pay. Kaysen and Turner imply that a "self-controlling" competitive process is the essence of the "invisible hand" (p. 48), but the coiner of that phrase used it otherwise—to characterize investment of capital where it would yield the most profit.

The distinctions drawn by writers who insist that firms must be "compelled along the only economically feasible line of conduct by the constraints of the market" (p. 15), but who condemn the "atomizing" of industry as fruitless and foolish, have to be subtle ones. This particular program might break up three, four, or five dominant companies in target industries into six, eight, or ten (compare p. 115). This is not atomization, but it will not give us the virtues of the all-powerful market either. Evidently the authors feel it will make industry *enough* more competitive to be worth the cost; one must accept this as the judgment of two specialists, but the logic is not so self-evident as to deny others the right to differ.

2. Bain's Evidence

Further support for the proposal is offered in Joe S. Bain's *Industrial Organization*. A recognized master in both economic and industry analysis, he develops here for his readers (including my own students) the following case against oligopoly: some concentrated industries (only "a significant minor fraction" of all industries) have shown (1) excessive profits, (2) excessive selling costs, or (3) poor product performance (p. 405). . . .

Excessive profits are said to exist whenever the net return on equity of all corporations is above the riskless rate of interest. For a single industry, this must be for a "prolonged period"—evidently a five-year average is in mind.

For the entire corporate sector, the year 1953, for example, showed total profits after taxes, less losses, equal to 7.8 percent of equity. Allowing for understatement of depreciation, this would be "excessive" by 2 or 3 percentage points. Net profits were 5.5 percent of national income (as in 1963 also), or excessive by perhaps 2 points (see pp. 382-84). The rest of society could indeed be grateful if owners of corporations would organize production for 60 or 65 percent of their present reward, and dissolution might give us a chance to test their willingness. If the effects on such financial institutions as pension trusts were more than just incidental, we might find ourselves regretting another experiment noble in purpose.

Kaysen and Turner consider a rate of interest adjusted to each industry's risk more appropriate than the riskless rate. They mention 6 to 8 percent on equity as a possible normal level of profits, and a 12 percent average over ten years as certainly "supernormal" (p. 63). In the First National City Bank's tabulation of published corporate reports, only 19 out of 65 industries were making less than 8 percent, or clearly normal, profits in 1962.

In Bain's treatment of individual industries, we are not (so far as I could find) told what "severe monopolistic restriction" (p. 386) he suspects to have caused the high profit rates of the 1953 leaders, for example—motor vehicles and equipment, electrical machinery and equipment, finance, chemicals, and tobacco manufactures. Such restrictions were not obvious in 1953, and are hardly so today.

It may be rigorous logic to say that risk taking is sufficiently

rewarded if profits above the pure rate of interest for some companies equal the deficiency in earnings by others. But are investors,
often anxious for gains and yet timid, so logical? One might try
telling them this:

If you are thinking of risking your money, bear in mind that an industry
profit averaging more than 4 percent over any five-year period may draw
public investigation. If your firm makes 5 or 6 percent, it will be excused
provided your competitors are making enough less than 4 percent to offset
it. Conversely, if other firms make more, we shall expect you to make less.

Even a logical investor might reflect that, while government
bonds are yielding 4 percent with complete safety, the same return
on a stock, at a liberal 75 percent payout, would yield only 3 percent cash income and with no guarantee. (If the company grows,
he should get his 1 percent and perhaps more back when he sells
his stock. There might be a tax benefit, which Kaysen and Turner
suggest reducing.)

Excessive selling costs are found principally in consumer products like cigarettes, liquor, soap, passenger cars, and gasoline. Can
a firm compete at all in such markets without incurring selling
expense, if the public fails to beat a path to its door as Emerson
once expected? Certainly we can reduce selling costs if we dis-
regard freedom to compete, as well as breadth of choice for consumers. But where is the evidence that we can reduce them by
doubling the number of firms?

New car dealerships and gasoline service stations, declared here
to be excessive in numbers, were distribution channels found by
these industries when earlier ones could not handle volume production of goods. Service stations, it is true, are often bunched near
each other, but motorists evidently prefer quick service to waiting
in line (admitted on p. 388, but not remembered on p. 392).

Poor product performance is "suspected" principally in (1) automobiles which are too "fancy" for the average purchaser, and (2)
these and other consumer durable goods whose frequent style
changes mean higher prices. When automobile styles change, an
economy-minded consumer may have to protect himself by keeping
his old model longer, or, when he replaces it, buying a second-hand
car. In a rich society, with rapid changes of public tastes, this type

of consumer cannot "call the tune" on products with luxury characteristics.

Does the non-oligopolistic women's dress industry do better in
the two respects criticized? It sells something more than a product
to keep out the cold, just as the motor industry sells something
more than transportation—and the food industry something more
than nutrition. . . .

F. CONCLUSION

Such is the evidence (unless I have missed something essential)
offered in two widely quoted books to support an antitrust campaign which appears, in this exposition, to be alien to our customary
economic and legal processes, and uncertain or even potentially
dangerous in its effects. I, at least, would like to see the evidence
strengthened and refined. . . .

PART IV

Other Antitrust Issues

ANTITRUST v. PATENTS

Laurence I. Wood

Laurence I. Wood is an attorney-at-law and Vice-President of the General Electric Company.

. . . The unique aspect of patent pools . . . is that the Supreme Court has been monotonously consistent from the time of its earliest decisions.

It is true, of course, that each new decision of the Supreme Court in the area surrounding problems of cooperation between patent owners, and the impact on that area of the antitrust laws, raises new fears and alarms lest the Court has cut away some substantial portion of its previously announced doctrines. But the fluctuations and the causes of concern have been mainly in peripheral areas; the main current of applicable law has been basically unaltered through half a century of litigious conflict.

In a very practical sense, this consistency is not surprising even in an era during which change has been the order of the day. . . . This singular unanimity can be explained in only one way—it has arisen through necessity. For, given our Federal patent laws, which provide for the issuance for a 17-year period of the right to exclude others from making, using or selling that which is the subject of the invention, the right to pool or interchange patent rights is absolutely essential. The reason for this is inherent in the very nature of the patent grant which gives to the inventor the right to exclude

The Record, XXI (1966), 625-635. Copyright 1966, Association of the Bar of the City of New York.

all others from his discovery. The first inventor in any field—Mr.
Fleming in the two-electrode vacuum tube—obtains, therefore, the
right to exclude everyone else. Now a second inventor, Mr. Lee De
Forest, two years later discovers an improvement on the original
discovery—the addition of a grid to the two-electrode vacuum tube,
permitting control of the flow of the electrons and constituting a
tremendous advance in the art—which improvement he patents. He
may now exclude everyone from the use of the improvement, but
he may not make or use it himself because to do so would infringe
on the original invention of Mr. Fleming. Thus, Mr. De Forest and
Mr. Fleming are at an impasse—neither may make the complete,
improved device. The monopolies are legally completely independent though they are given on inventions wholly interdependent.
This situation is legally difficult to avoid; it is economically impossible to tolerate.

Inasmuch as there has been no legislative solution, avoidance of
serious deadlocks throughout the entire economy lies only in positive
action by the conflicting patentees. It is here that the element of
cooperation enters into the patent system. The logical and necessary
procedure is either to unite or to share the right to use both patents,
so that the complete product may be manufactured and sold. If
this is done by uniting the two patents into one ownership, it becomes a patent pool. If the sharing is done by means of an exchange
of licenses—each patentee licensing the other under his invention
—this becomes a cross license. Cooperation among patent owners
thus serves the purpose of eliminating restrictions between mutually
obstructive patents. In its ideal form, the pool or interchange thus
serves not to restrain competition but to permit it. The original inventor receives the right to use the improvement invention, and
the improvement inventor the right to use the original invention.
The result is that where before each had only the negative right
to exclude the other, both may now make the complete product
in its perfected form. . . .

Let me take a moment for . . . a definition of our terms. "Patent
pool" has been used to include situations ranging from elaborate
patent holding and research arrangements to a simple cross license.
For our purposes today, the most satisfactory definition of a patent
pool is that it comprises all modes and forms of cooperation between patents held by different interests. While, strictly speaking,

a pool exists only where title to patents is transferred, the considerations present in cross-licensing agreements are virtually identical; therefore the two modes of patent cooperation will be treated as synonymous. The methods of effecting the cooperation may be of several types: the most common is by means of cross licenses; another is to assign all patents to a trustee who in turn gives each member a license under the combined patents. Often the result is achieved by purchase or assignment; occasionally by a consolidation of two or more concerns. But whatever the device, and whatever its ultimate aims, the immediate object is to free the members, to some extent at least, from the exclusions of the combined patents.

The need and desirability of patent pools, and the dangers inherent in the use of such pools, have been recognized and illuminated by a wealth of authority. Patent pools are desirable and beneficial where they resolve patent conflicts and make the pooled patents available to others, facilitate licensing of large numbers of patents, or make feasible the practice of the inventions of mutually dependent or conflicting patents. The Supreme Court [in the *Standard Oil (Ind.)* case] observed that patent pooling may thus promote rather than restrain competition.

Conversely, patent pooling, involving as it does agreement and cooperation, may open the door to unreasonable restraint of trade and monopolization. And it has long been settled [since the *Standard Sanitary* case in 1912] that the presence of patents does not provide immunity to industry-wide regimentation, or to agreements to exclude competitors from specified markets.

It is clear at the outset then that a patent pool is not improper in itself. It is equally clear, however, that improper motivation or misuse through restraint, monopolization or the like, may cause the pool to become unlawful under the Sherman Act.

Problems of patent interchanges are complicated on several fronts. In the first place, by definition, a pool involves in one form or another a concentration of patents, a bringing together of a number of separately held monopolies. Sometimes this concentration of patents is accompanied or is fostered by or among large companies, thereby incorporating the ubiquitous aspect of size into the problem. Secondly, patent pools, again by definition, invariably involve agreements between different patent owners, and these agreements may themselves present problems of a possible trade-restraining nature. Third, very practical problems arise as to the making available to others, who are not members of the pool, of rights to use the patents included in the pool. Finally, in recent years pools have been brought under examination not so much as part of a direct attack against the patent holding itself, but as a concomitant to an attack on the alleged monopoly position of the patent owners. . . .

1. CONCENTRATION OF PATENTS

Few problems in the antitrust area are considered in a vacuum. It is almost inevitable that when a court considers the propriety of any patent arrangement, many factors weigh heavily in the court's determination. When any company or group of companies manages a number of significant patents, one of the first questions antitrust-wise is in connection with their acquisition. Certainly the acquisition of a patent by the inventor or the employer as assignee through the issuance by the Patent Office does not give rise to any antitrust problem, even where the acquisition is accompanied by a specific intent not to use the patent. Questions may arise, however . . . where the patent acquisition is by purchase, whether from a competitor, from an independent inventor, or through a grant-back clause in a license agreement. The problems become complex where the acquisition by a single company covers substantially all the patents in a key field. There the inquiry centers on whether the acquisition was by patent grant or through purchase; whether it is from a competitor, and the nature of the accompanying intent or purpose of the acquisition. Size, and the fact of size, are also important considerations in connection with such a concentration of patents.

It has been obviously true for many years that there is a widely variant norm of conduct for companies in a dominant position as against those which are not. Many difficult problems, however, arise when several companies holding important patents enter into agreements with each other.

2. PATENT AGREEMENTS

The waiver of mutually obstructive patent roadblocks by interchange agreements is one of the essentials to progress in our highly integrated industrial economy. However, it is at once apparent that there are in such exchanges all the troublesome problems inherent in every relationship between competitors. As is so frequent in the patent antitrust arena, the abuse of an otherwise perfectly proper device may very quickly subject it to censure. The patent interchange agreement is dangerous where it is used not to create patent freedom but rather to add to the exclusivity of each patent the exclusion of conspiracy. It is here that patent combinations come into direct conflict with the Sherman Act. The device of the pool magnifies and sensitizes all the usual antitrust problems already inherent in patent administration. It possesses also the additional conflicts of the new court-evolved rules of inference and conspiracy.

Accordingly, throughout the early cases and the recent ones alike there are two fundamental assumptions forming an identifiable pattern: the clear recognition of the need for interchange; the eternal vigilance for any restrictive features which produce anti-competitive rather than liberalizing consequences. Consequently the fact that the Supreme Court has been consistent in its fundamental philosophy does not, unfortunately, make particularly simple the problem of the patent owners who desire to make effective utilization of a group of patents.

Certainly the first thing that any court will consider . . . is the purpose of the patent interchange. In the field of blocking patents— of the sort illustrated previously where the existence of each patent precludes the utilization of the other—the law has long been established that the existence of a bone fide dispute justifies a pooling arrangement. In *Standard Oil Company (Ind.)* v. *United States,* the Court approved an arrangement in which three large gasoline producers and one licensing concern pooled their conflicting, competing patents and agreed upon royalties to be charged and how those royalties would be divided. As to the charge that competition in the licensing of patents was eliminated, the Court noted that each of the four participants was free to license under its own or any pooled patent. The Court emphasized the necessity of patent interchange for technological advancement and the fact that, where licenses are available, pooling promotes rather than restrains competition.

Sometimes patents are pooled which do not conflict with each other in the terms of blocking utilization but which do cover related or complementary equipment. Pools of such complementary patents have been approved as a reasonable means of exploiting the patent monopolies and making them available for use. In their search for the relevant purpose, courts may derive their notions of the framers' original intent from their analysis of the practices of the pool in action: if the effect is to regiment an industry, to fix prices, or to forestall competition through threats of patent litigation, an illegal purpose will be presumed.

One distinctive aspect of cross licensing or patent interchange is through interference settlement agreements. As Mr. Justice White has explained in his concurring opinion in *United States* v. *Singer,* "In cases where several applicants claim the same subject matter the Patent Office declares an interference. This is an adversary proceeding between the rival applicants, primarily for the purpose of determining relative priority." These interference proceedings involving as they do the taking of testimony, the filing of briefs, the making of arguments, are, like any litigation, expensive. Furthermore, there is considerable risk to either of the parties lest an adverse outcome deprive him completely of his right to claim the subject invention. Understandably, therefore, it not infrequently happens that there will be interference settlements arrived at in advance by the parties sometimes providing that whoever prevails will grant the other a license under the forthcoming patent. More importantly the parties sometimes agree to the interference settlement without going through the litigious step at all. In these instances they devise some means for determining which party shall be the successful one and provide for a sharing of the subsequent patent rights with the unsuccessful party. . . .

Because of the potentiality for abuse present in the situation, Congress a few years ago required that all interference settlement agreements must be filed with the Patent Office.

It is in the industry-wide multilateral licensing arrangements that we confront the situation normally thought of as a patent pool. Here are represented some of the most salutary benefits of patent interchanges—where entire industries have during the formative stages made available their patent rights to any applicant. Well known examples are the Automobile Manufacturers Association and the Manufacturers Aircraft Association. But multilateral licenses also involve, by their nature, the problem of inter-company cooperation. And since the days of Judge Gary it has been assumed that men who come to dinner remain to enjoy a conspiracy.

Quite obviously in this area, interchange agreements would be illegal where they constitute no more than corporate treaties carving out exclusive areas of an industry for each member company. Throughout the history of the antitrust laws, restrictive combinations of patents have been consistently recognized as being far beyond the scope of the protection afforded by the patent laws, and altogether subject to the Sherman Act. Consistent with economic need there can be, and there is, no objection to the creation of pools to which access is ready and free from arbitrary restraints. There is no objection to provisions for specified royalties so long as the provisions do not provide a cloak for price control or restraint of trade. And, in the absence of other factors indicative of restraint of trade, the centralized conduct of infringement suits is permissible.

Here again there is and can be no rigid rule. The only sensible approach to the problem of the validity of patent interchange agreements is through the Rule of Reason type of examination. . . . The *Standard Oil of Indiana* case . . . is a classic example of this approach as applied to the legality of patent pools.

The nature of the pooled patents is an important consideration in determining the purpose and the legality of the pool. If they are non-competing patents, no competition between them has been eliminated. Illegality will arise only through restrictive practices, and the burden of proving illegality should rest upon the one asserting it. Where the patents are competing, the pool may serve to eliminate competition between the patent holders, if in fact there has been such competition. In such case the purpose of the pool becomes a highly important question. Where the patents are obviously weak or invalid, and the interchange simply a means of protecting them from attack, it will be struck down. Where competing patents are involved, it would appear that if the one asserting illegality of the pool proves that competition between the patent holders had heretofore existed but had been eliminated through the formation of the pool, then the burden of going forward with proof as to the propriety of the pool under the Rule of Reason should shift to the members of the pool. Avoidance of patent conflict, making patents easily available to the industry through a common source and like propositions would be pertinent to that burden.

The position in the industry of the participants may bear upon the possibility of pool abuse. However, in no event should that position determine the validity of the pool. Rather, the nature and importance of the pooled patents, the royalty and licensing policies, the uses of the pool, the presence or absence of vigorously used litigation funds, the presence or absence of a "common front threat" to non-members, and similar pertinent factors must be considered. So long as there is an open licensing pool, free from restrictions, the pool should not be held unlawful. In all events, the pool should not be held illegal, irrespective of the existence of monopoly power unless upon the fullest application of the Rule of Reason the purpose or operation is found to be unreasonable. Uniform judicial application of the Rule of Reason, supported by an enlightened enforcement policy in the Department of Justice, should suffice to assure the desired results.

3. LICENSING UNDER POOLED PATENTS

Where a single company has decided that it will issue licenses under its patent holdings, it first faces the perplexing problem as to what type of licensing structure should be created. The problem is particularly perplexing where the patents involved are numerous and dominant in an industry. Here are raised policy and legal questions as to licenses under future patents, exclusive licenses, limitations as to quantity, time, territory or field of use, and, if the client is particularly hardy and litigious, limitations as to price. Grouping these all together, it is true of each of them that there is no decision holding such a license in itself is a violation of the antitrust laws. However, a word of caution is essential here. In each of these situations the underlying assumption of the court was that it was dealing with a case involving only the validity of the licensing provisions; in none was the attack centered on the charge that the device was used as part of an underlying conspiracy to restrain or eliminate competition in the industry involved.

When two patent owners enter into a cross-license agreement exchanging rights under their respective patents, the question as to the obligation to grant licenses to others and the question as to the nature of such licenses becomes more complex. Certainly where the object made under the cross-licensed patents is relatively unimportant, or where the companies are not dominant in the field involved, there would seem to be no requirement to grant licenses to others; the situation may be otherwise, however, where the parties between themselves control virtually the entire market. One of the most neglected portions of the opinion in *United States* v. *National Lead Company* (and that which is for our purposes perhaps most important) is that which pertains to the domestic cross-license agreement between National Lead and Du Pont. Although the Court held the agreement illegal as part of the entire international conspiracy involved in that case, Mr. Justice Burton hinted in a dictum that any cross license between two dominant companies is bad *per se*, without any restrictive limitations, if the patents are not made available to others. [p. 319]

Where industry-wide, multilateral licensing arrangements are involved, I believe it only sensible and consistent with sound practice to make advance provisions for licensing others on reasonable terms. The arrangements which thus extend patent licenses under the pooled patents should be considered from the standpoint of the practical reasons which dictate the advisability of the patent pool, from the standpoint of the scope and character of the patents involved, and from the standpoint of the economic effects of the agreements. Where the agreements are reasonably related to the character of the patents and to the legitimate reasons for the pool, they should be upheld. Where they go further and restrain competitive activity beyond the extent reasonably required by the patent situation, the agreements should be proscribed. Price fixing provisions in agreements relating to patent pools . . . inherently extend beyond the scope of the patent and into the area of joint action. They would, accordingly, be regarded as violations of the antitrust law. Where a patent pool combines patent rights in such a way as to dominate an industry—the domination coming through the fact of the combination—licenses should be made uniformly available to every member of the industry. It should not be material that the distribution of royalties among pool members fails to reflect exactly the value of the pooled patent rights. Finally, non-competitors should be free to engage in joint research and to divide the resultant patent rights in accord with their respective fields of activity.

4. IMPLICATING FACTORS

Our consideration of the problems of the patent pools thus far has
been along lines of the traditional test tube or vacuum approach to
antitrust problems involving a patent pool. Under such an approach,
I submit, an analysis of the applicable legal principles is relatively
simple once the relevant facts have been ascertained. From time to
time, indeed, patent antitrust cases do still arise as rather classic
laboratory-type studies in which patent practices are considered by
themselves as being the heart of the antitrust proceedings. Cases
such as *Hartford Empire, Ethyl Gasoline, Gypsum, General Electric*
[1926] and *National Lead* centered around these companies' acquisitions and their use of their patent property. In this area the
courts have engaged for several decades in a new "formulation" of
law, first conclusively determining that patents and patent practices
were not, as had originally been thought, basically immune from
antitrust prosecution, and second, defining in a case-by-case examination and with varying degrees of clarity just which patent
practices were proper and which improper. . . .

But I submit that in today's antitrust enforcement program, and
particularly in the area encompassing patent combinations or patent
pools, the classic patent antitrust decisions are only secondarily important. The important point of some of the new antitrust cases is
the emphasis on charges of monopolization and conspiracy in which
the use of patents or patent licenses is factored in as one of a
number of elements considered by the court. . . .

Let me clarify the distinction which I am drawing. In traditional
patent-antitrust cases the Department of Justice and the courts seek
to obtain a judicial clarification of what a patentee may or may not
do as a proper exercise of his patent rights. For example, on last
year's Supreme Court docket there was an attempt at obtaining
such a "clarification" in the Department of Justice effort to have the
patent license portion of the 1926 *General Electric* case overruled.

But under the new comprehensive approach, the examination is
whether a company or a group of companies have improperly restrained trade or monopolized an industry through their overall
activities. Various aspects of those activities may be pricing activities, the buying up of competitors, participating in trade associations, patent suits, patent licenses, etc. Obviously, in such an ex-

amination, emphasis on the black or white of what is permissible in patent license limitations as a naked proposition of law loses some of its significance. For here the ancient doctrine that devices ever so proper in themselves may be improperly used services as a leveling medium.

I should like to consider . . . briefly the manner in which the courts have thus turned to an examination of patent practices not as an end in themselves, but as makeweights or determinative factors in considering a larger guilt or innocence. We shall find, in reversal of the staid mathematical proposition, that the whole is sometimes greater than the sum of its parts.

Perhaps the most troublesome area wherein the existence of a patent interchange or patent pool may be brought to bear upon an antitrust inquiry is in connection with Section 2 of the Sherman Act, which prohibits the monopolization of any part of any industry or any conspiracy or any attempt to monopolize. As a starter, the very presence of patents in a monopolization case presents semantic problems. For it is inevitable where one is trying to determine the presence or absence of an illegal monopoly that one cannot escape the psychological import of words such as "monopoly," "exclusive," "restricted," and allied expressions which are part and parcel of patent terminology, and yet which are most troublesome in the arena of Section 2 of the Act. For when one starts with the more recent interpretations of Section 2—to the effect that all that need be shown in addition to market dominance is that the dominance was achieved by other than inevitable economic means—even an ancient history of patent purchases, exclusive licenses, limited licensing, or patent interchange agreements could propel the patent owner into the area of illegality.

It is for this reason that Judge Knox was careful in the *Carboloy* [*General Electric* case in 1948] case to observe that "although in a non-patent case, exclusion, unlawful achievement, and cause of monopoly power may not need to be proved, elements of such conduct are necessary in a patent case before Section 2 may be invoked." [p. 1015] The difficulty, however, is that the activities of the patentee in enforcing statutory rights are in their very nature exclusive, so that a perpetual semantic dilemma entails. Furthermore, practices which under the interpretations of one day may be neither unlawful nor abusive, often become so under subsequent judicial interpretations of the law. The too frequent disposition of the courts is to use this after acquired knowledge as a criterion by which to judge the patentee's prior conduct. Thus, there is a very realistic sense in which the fact of ownership of patents may today in some circumstances become more of a hazard from the standpoint of antitrust prosecution than it is a defense.

Another troublesome aspect of patent problems as related to Section 2 is in connection with the definition of the market alleged to be monopolized. There is a very real temptation to the enforcement officials to consider the area of the patent itself as being the field to be measured for monopoly. Quite obviously, if the patent in question is of any value or strength, this would mean automatically that the area of commerce involved is always monopolized by the patentee.

Under such an approach, if the patents are broad and significant, there is, as Judge Knox observed in the *Carboloy* case, no question of whether defendants have "monopolized." In that case he said, "Here the patents defined a whole new industry. The defendants admit to monopoly. The defense is that the monopoly was lawful, coming within the protection of the patent grants. Decision must turn on whether or not the patent privilege has been misused." [p. 1015]

There is thus considerable danger that within the interweaving of the issues, normal patent licensing practices will when later considered take on new and sinister portent so that the very terminology of patent practice could be confused with illegality. And if each patent were to be construed as making its owner dominant and monopolistic within the marketing area for his own patented article, the *reductio ad absurdum* would be that every patentee would be called upon to give a rigorous accounting for his motives and his conduct.

In the words of the Attorney General's National Committee to Study the Antitrust Laws, "The inevitable result of lawful use of a lawful patent monopoly is not to be penalized."

Fortunately the Supreme Court at its last term has indicated a thorough understanding of the danger of this semantic confusion in *Walker Process Equipment* v. *Food Machinery Corp.* The alleged infringer contended that where a patent has been obtained fraudulently from the Patent Office and is subsequently knowingly as-

serted against others in the industry, this establishes a *per se* monopolization or attempt to monopolize in violation of Section 2. In
answering this contention Mr. Justice Clark for the Court made it
explicitly clear that there is no such *per se* rule and that true market dominance is the test: "To establish monopolization . . . under
section 2 of the Sherman Act, it would then be necessary to appraise
the exclusionary power of the illegal patent claim in terms of the
relevant market for the produce involved. . . . It may be that the
device . . . does not comprise a relevant market. There may be
effective substitutes for the device which do not infringe the patent."

CONCLUSION

I, for one, contend that the only proper approach to an analysis of
the validity of the interchange agreements is through the Rule of
Reason type of examination demonstrated in the *Standard Oil of
Indiana* case. It is true that in large areas of the problem of relationships with competitors the doctrine of unreasonable *per se* has
become the order of the day—the court enunciating one new formula after another for shortcutting, minimizing and finally eliminating evidence as to the economic impact of the challenged arrangement. Thus it has been with agreements fixing prices, minimum or
maximum, with types of tying clauses, of requirements contracts, of
boycotts.

I am confident that as to the validity of patent arrangements the
court will continue to follow the cogent words of Mr. Justice Brandeis in the *Gasoline Cracking* [*Standard Oil* (*Ind.*)] case "that where
owners of conflicting or complementary patents seek in good faith
to free the art for all participants so that the barricades of patents
will no longer bar the way," [p. 164] the court, if called upon to
test the device, will do so in the full light of all the facts as to reasonableness, as to availability, as to dominance, as to restrictiveness,
as to necessity or desirability, as to impact on the market, on the
product, on the price, and on source. This is the teaching of the Rule
of Reason as applied to patent interchange; it is compatible with the
economic objectives of effective competition. It is the only assurance
of achieving a workable antitrust law and workable competition. . . .

Governmental policy, I submit, should first, assert the desirability and importance of achieving new discoveries, and second, encourage and foster the interchange of the rights to the ready use of those discoveries.

The patent system is the basic medium of the Government's encouragement of inventive achievement and of the investments essential to such invention. Since this is so, the interchange of patent rights is the only feasible way of encouraging cooperative progress of science and useful arts, and of achieving the full play of competitive vigor in our economy. No rigid standard of preordained rectitude is available for giving guidance for such exchanges. There is no absolute of right or wrong. Rather the resolution must continue to be through an adult case-by-case application of the standards of effective competition in accordance with the realities of economic life.

FRANCHISING AND BUSINESS INDEPENDENCE

Milton Handler

Milton Handler is Professor of Law at the Columbia Law School. Among his numerous publications are the annual surveys of anti- trust law that appear in The Record, *the monthly publication of the Association of the Bar of the City of New York.*

The franchise method of distribution has, in recent years, become the subject of considerable debate in the business community. Since the advent of what has been called the "franchise boom," the busi- ness literature has been replete with discussion of this multifaceted method of marketing. And the courts have increasingly been called upon the reexamine long standing doctrines regulating the extent to which a business with a product, a process or a trademark may organize their distribution and use. The Supreme Court, in review- ing [in *White Motor*] the validity of two of the arrangements com- monly utilized in franchising, has stated that "we do not know enough of the economic and business stuff out of which these ar- rangements emerge" to be able to decide whether they should be tested under the rule of reason or treated as perniciously anticom- petitive and thus *per se* unlawful. [p. 263]

Franchise arrangements . . . are divisible into two categories: (1) the issuance of a franchise to a distributor or dealer who may handle other products as well as those of the franchisor and customarily does business under his own trade name; and (2) the franchising of entire business enterprises in which the franchisee operates his busi- ness under the franchisor's trade name, is identified as a member of

Originally published under the title of "Statement Before the Small Business Administration" in *The Antitrust Bulletin,* XI (1966), 417-437. Copyright 1966, Federal Legal Publications.

a select group of dealers, and generally is required to follow standardized or prescribed methods of operation. . . .

Let us first examine the question from the point of view of the franchisor. . . . If the manufacturer has substantial financial resources, it may integrate forward and distribute the product itself through its own branches. But companies which lack the capital to expand into distribution must find other business entities to handle their products in the marketplace, and franchising permits this on the broadest possible scale without the necessity for inordinate capital expenditure. Moreover, to the extent that the manufacturer faces competition from an integrated company, the establishment of franchises allows him to compete vigorously on a more nearly equal footing, providing him with the ingenuity and incentive of the small businessmen who receive his franchise, and permitting him to utilize the numerous tools of modern merchandising which might otherwise be unavailable to a company of limited means. . . .

From the franchisee's point of view, the franchise system creates opportunities for small businessmen unparalleled in the economy today. By means of franchising, a small businessman with limited resources and limited experience can, under the aegis of the franchisor, become an independent entrepreneur with a reasonable expectation of success. The usual franchise arrangement, particularly when an entire business enterprise is franchised, provides guidance for the franchisee in the form of standards, tested operating methods and marketing techniques as well as experienced internal procedures. Since most retail failures result from inexperience, incompetence and other factors related to management qualifications, the franchisee is much more likely than his nonfranchised counterpart to be able to make a success of his business. . . .

The current ferment in the law with respect to franchise distribution has focused on the variety of restrictions utilized in franchise agreements. There are a number of these restrictions, to be found in various combinations from case to case. I shall limit my remarks to five which I think are fairly illustrative of the legal and business problems involved:

1. Exclusive Selling;
2. Exclusive Buying;

3. Territorial Restrictions;
4. Customer Restrictions; and
5. Quality Control of Trademarked Products.

. . . These restrictions . . . are all, of course, restraints of trade; their very purpose, after all, is to restrain. But this does not make them unlawful. . . . Under the rule of reason . . . it is necessary to show that they unreasonably restrain trade before they are placed beyond the pale of the Sherman Act. The important fact is that, when examined from the broad perspective of competition in the market as a whole, these restraints are more often than not pro-competitive because they strengthen interbrand competition and foster small business units.

These are not novel restraints. The restrictions in modern franchise agreements all have antecedents in nineteenth and early twentieth century business practices, and a vast body of doctrine, both at common law and under the antitrust statutes, has developed. In the course of the law's evolution, most of these restraints have been upheld as reasonable in light of their business justifications. . . .

1. *Exclusive Selling*—Many franchise arrangements include a provision whereby the seller or franchisor promises the buyer or franchisee that he will not sell the product to anyone else in the franchisee's defined territory. The restraint, in short, is on the seller. Such restrictions, often called exclusive franchises or exclusive agencies, serve several important functions. From the seller's viewpoint, he is able, by keeping the number of middlemen-buyers to a minimum, to reduce his selling costs; and, by selecting only the most solvent dealer in each area, he is able to limit his credit risk. But more important, such an exclusive arrangement will often be absolutely necessary in order to induce a dealer to accept the product. Especially when the product is new or its distribution requires a substantial selling expense or a large initial investment in showroom, service facilities and the like, the manufacturer may be unable to obtain adequate dealer distribution without affording assurances that the dealer will not be faced with direct competition, in close geographical proximity, from the manufacturer himself or from some other franchisee appointed for the same territory. . . . The distribu-

tor, faced with effective competition from other brands, will be hesitant to take on the product without such protection from intrabrand competition.

These business reasons for exclusive representation arrangements have, in large measure, been accepted by the courts. The law in this area has derived essentially from the common law doctrines of ancillary restraints, more particularly from those rules governing covenants not to compete ancillary to the sale of a business. . . .

The ancillary restraints rule, as it has been applied to exclusive selling agreements, has become synonymous with the absence of monopoly or market dominance. If the seller is dominant in the market, or if the buyer attempts to achieve such dominance, the restriction is deemed unreasonable. But when market dominance is not present, and other buyers have available to them the products of other suppliers, exclusive representation arrangements have been upheld.

The courts have also been aware of the peculiar needs of the small businessman respecting exclusive representation. Since the principal reason for the restraint is to provide assurance against intrabrand competition to a dealer who must invest his capital and his energies in building a market for the product, the smaller the manufacturer, the more likely it is that such assurances from the seller will be required. This was noted by the United States Court of Appeals for the District of Columbia in the *Packard* case:

The short of it is that a relatively small manufacturer, competing with large manufacturers, thought it advantageous to retain its largest dealer in Baltimore, and could not do so without agreeing to drop its other Baltimore dealers. To penalize the small manufacturer for competing in this way not only fails to promote the policy of the antitrust laws but defeats it. [p. 421]

. . . 2. *Exclusive Buying*—Another restriction often found in franchise arrangements is the so-called exclusive buying or dealing provision whereby the dealer is required to purchase only the seller's products to the exclusion of rival brands. There the restraint is on the franchisee. Such agreements can have serious anticompetitive effects in that they may deny competitors reasonable access to supplies or markets. But they can also serve useful business purposes. The franchisor may be able to increase his sales and obtain better service for customers by selling to dealers who must focus all of their sales and promotional efforts on his brand. In addition, the dealer handling only one supplier's products is likely to carry a full stock rather than a limited number of items. Furthermore, when the exclusive arrangement takes the form of a requirements contract, as is often the case, the franchisor may be able to reduce his selling expenses, achieve protection against fluctuations in price, improve his ability to predict the scope of his market and, particularly in the case of a smaller company, enable himself to compete on a stronger footing with his larger competitors. And when an exclusive selling arrangement is contemplated, an exclusive buying provision can constitute a vital *quid pro quo* to avoid placing the seller at the dealer's mercy.

Exclusive buying arrangements can also be of substantial value to the dealer who is subject to the restriction. For example, Justice Frankfurter has pointed out that, "they may assure supply, afford protection against rises in price, enable long-term planning on the basis of known costs, and obviate the expense and risk of storage in the quantity necessary for a commodity having a fluctuating demand." [p. 314]

The law's treatment of exclusive dealing arrangements has had a long history marked by sharp swings of the pendulum from extreme positions both of legality and invalidity. In the early years under the Sherman Act they were viewed with general favor, except when accompanied by an external unlawful purpose such as an attempt to monopolize or a price-fixing scheme. Then, with the passage of Section 3 of the Clayton Act, Congress dealt specifically with the problem and prohibited those exclusives which are likely to substantially lessen competition. Under this statutory rubric, the rules continued to fluctuate. In *Standard-Magrane* the emphasis was placed on the seller's market dominance. But in the *Standard* [*Oil (Calif.)*] decision of 1949, the Supreme Court fashioned a rule of quantitative substantiality which automatically proscribed all exclusive dealing arrangements which foreclosed competition in a substantial share of the market, the Court holding that 6.7% was sufficiently substantial. More recently, in the *Tampa Electric* case in 1961, the Court brought the pendulum back to a more realistic balance, explicitly requiring an examination of the probable impact of the exclusive on competition in a properly defined market:

To determine substantiality in a given case, it is necessary to weigh the probable effect of the contract on the relevant area of effective competition, taking into account the relative strength of the parties, the proportionate volume of commerce involved in relation to the total volume of commerce in the relevant market area, and the probable immediate and future effects which pre-emption of that share of the market might have on effective competition therein. It follows that a mere showing that the contract itself involves a substantial number of dollars is ordinarily of little consequence. [p. 329]

Since the *Tampa* decision, this rationale has been generally followed.

The important lesson to be learned from this history is that a restriction such as an exclusive dealing agreement should not be outlawed merely because it has some anticompetitive effects. Only when the likely impact of the restraint on the market as a whole is analyzed can a proper and economically realistic result be reached. The interests of small business should not be underestimated in this realm. As Justice Douglas cogently pointed out in his *Standard [Oil (Calif.)]* dissent, the elimination of restrictions such as requirements contracts from distribution schemes utilizing small independent dealers may well lead to increased vertical integration and the ultimate elimination of small business. No doubt, some exclusive dealing arrangements are capable of producing serious anticompetitive results; but there are no easy shortcuts which can avoid the painstaking analysis needed to determine when an arrangement should be outlawed. . . .

3. *Territorial Restrictions*—The restriction which has probably evoked more comment than any other in recent years is the one whereby a franchisor limits the geographic territory in which the franchisee to whom he sells may resell the product. These restrictions, found in many franchising arrangements, are predicated on business reasons quite similar to those underlying exclusive representation arrangements; and . . . serve a similar role in fostering interbrand competition.

Territorial restrictions take many forms but can generally be divided into two types: "closed territories" in which the dealer is prohibited from soliciting sales in another's territory but may nevertheless sell to any customer who comes to his place of business; and "geographical customer allocation" in which the dealer is permitted to sell only to those customers who reside or have a place of business in his territory. Both types of restraint serve essentially the same economic function.

The primary problem facing a non-integrated manufacturer is to arrange for the distribution of his product by independent dealers which will result in optimum sales and consumer acceptance. Accordingly, it is imperative that he obtain dealers who are willing and able to provide the necessary promotion, advertising and service. Sellers often find it difficult to get dealers willing to undertake the risks inherent in distribution without some guarantee that their efforts will bear fruit. This is particularly true when the product requires large advertising expenditures and consistent expansion of distribution facilities; when substantial pre-sale effort is necessary; when after-sale service is an important element in maintaining the product's good will; or when the product has not achieved a high level of consumer acceptance. . . .

Moreover, if the seller desires to achieve maximum market penetration, he must encourage his dealers to exploit the potential of their territories to the fullest possible extent. By overextending himself into neighboring territories a dealer may spread himself too thin and adequate representation in the home area will suffer. Furthermore, the temptation to steal the easy sale from his neighboring dealer—"skimming the cream"—may cause the more difficult sale at home to be lost to the competing brand and, even more important, the neighboring dealer who needs some "cream" to sustain his business may be forced to drop the product from his line as unprofitable. This is particularly so when the product requires pre-selling. . . . And when after-sale service is important, the local dealer may not do as good a job of servicing a product sold by someone else, the net result being customer dissatisfaction.

Territorial restrictions. . . . also enhance competition on the dealer side of the distribution equation. If such protection from intrabrand competition is not available, only the larger, more financially secure dealers could afford to assume the expenses of taking on the line. The small retailer would be very wary of spending large sums on advertising or investing considerable funds in sales personnel and service merely to build a market for someone else to take away. . . .

The courts have generally been receptive to these business justifications in assessing the legality of territorial restrictions. Both at common law and under the Sherman Act these restraints have been sustained when, after an examination of the pertinent market facts, they have been found reasonable. But commencing in 1949 the Department of Justice announced that it viewed such restrictions as illegal *per se*. The Government has, since that time, obtained a large number of consent decrees enjoining territorial restraints without having to subject its legal theory to judicial scrutiny. It is noteworthy that the other agency charged with antitrust enforcement, the Federal Trade Commission, has not taken such an extreme approach and has treated territorial restrictions under the rule of reason. Consent decrees, of course, are not precedents and do not establish binding rules of law.

The problem finally came to the Supreme Court in the *White Motor* case, but the Court declined to say whether territorial restrictions were *per se* unlawful, holding that their legality should be determined only after a full trial. In a concurring opinion, Justice Brennan suggested that it would be pertinent to inquire whether the restraint was more restrictive than necessary, assuming that some restraint was justified on the facts. . . .

. . . The decided cases make it plain that these restraints are to be judged under the rule of reason. To be sure, if the genesis of the restriction is horizontal in nature—that is, if it is spawned by dealers acting in concert who then prevail upon their supplier to "impose" it on them—there is a horizontal agreement to divide territories which is unlawful *per se*. But such a horizontal genesis must be proved by extrinsic evidence, not presumed just because the business interest of the supplier in establishing an effective marketing organization happens to coincide with the wishes of the dealers.

As for the suggestion that a franchisor must show that he couldn't have managed with a less restrictive alternative, such a rule would impose an impractical if not impossible burden. Once a franchisor shows that he was justified, by sound business reasons, in imposing territorial restrictions on his dealers, how, as a practical matter, can he go on to show, after the fact, that some other arrangement would not have served the same end? . . . The important thing to note about territorial restrictions is that, despite the Justice Department's extreme position, the courts have recognized the strong business reasons underlying them and have made it clear that, when reasonable, they are lawful. . . .

4. *Customer Restrictions*—In the constant battle to better their position in the interbrand competitive struggle, franchisors have imposed restrictions on their dealers governing the types of customers to whom they can resell the franchisor's product. These arrangements, like the others I have discussed, are predicated on sound business justifications.

Customer limitations take a variety of forms. The franchisor may wish to deal directly with certain large accounts, such as the federal government, state and local governments and customers with numerous outlets who do their purchasing through central agencies. In such cases, inability to deal with the customer centrally may result in losing the sale to a competitor, especially when large inventory, delivery and installation to widely separated locations and after-sale service and maintenance are required. If the dealer were to make the sale because of a low price and not provide proper service or promotional work, it would be the product's reputation which would suffer.

On the other hand, the manufacturer may decide to reserve no sales to himself, but seek to channel the sales of certain dealers to certain types of customers. This provides for orderly distribution to particular classes of customers—just as the territorial restriction does on a geographical basis. The manufacturer's purpose is to maximize sales and render optimum service through dealers who are able to concentrate their efforts on the special classes of trade which they are best equipped to handle. The franchisor may also seek to enhance his position vis-à-vis other brands by limiting wholesalers to sales to retailers, or to retailers approved by the manufacturer, as well as by restricting retailers to sales to consumers.

The law regarding customer restrictions is much the same as that applicable to the territorial variety. The great majority of the cases have sustained the limitation when found reasonable in the economic circumstances. The Justice Department has viewed them as unlawful *per se* and the Supreme Court, in *White Motor,* left the question open. . . .

5. *Quality Controls*—The central element of most franchises of entire enterprises is a license granted the franchisee to use the franchisor's trademark or trade name. This right to do business under a well known brand name is usually the single most valuable asset acquired by a franchisee with his franchise. As a condition of the

license, most franchise agreements require the franchisee to buy his products from the franchisor. When the product is not ready-made but must be manufactured by the franchisee, the condition generally relates to the ingredients to be used. Standards of service, production and advertising are also often prescribed in the agreement.

As is the case with the other restrictions . . . these conditions are restraints upon the freedom of the independent franchisee to run his business as he sees fit. But they are particularly essential to the success of a franchise operation and are frequently necessary as a matter of law to protect the value of the franchisor's trademark. . . .

The greatest advantage available to a franchisee is a well-known trademark under which he is able to capitalize on advertising and merchandising on a scale well beyond the means of an ordinary independent merchant and to enter the market with a certain degree of consumer acceptance assured. But this advantage is available only so long as the public can be certain that the quality of the product it buys at any franchised outlet is uniform and meets the standard universally set by the franchisor's brand throughout the market.

Similarly, the supplier is able to utilize franchise distribution successfully only if he can maintain the quality of the products sold under his trademark. If the quality of the product is not uniform among all his dealers, his chances for continued success are likely to be substantially lessened. Thus rigid standards of quality control must be imposed upon franchisees as a matter of business necessity.

But the requirement that the franchisee buy his products or their essential ingredients from the franchisor or approved sources is essential for another reason, deriving from the very nature of a trademark. . . . The trademark indicates the source or origin of goods symbolizing the reputation and good will of the owner's business. It also protects the public by offering assurance that the product is genuine. Accordingly, both at common law and under the Lanham Act, a trademark license is valid only if the licensor exercises control over the nature and quality of the licensee's product.

Thus, when a franchisor requires his licensee to purchase the trademarked product or its ingredients from him or an approved source, he not only guaranties a uniform product of established quality to the public, but he also engages in the quality control necessary to maintain his trademark rights. . . .

This brief review of some of the restrictions typically utilized in franchise arrangements demonstrates several important facts about this marketing phenomenon. Society has a vital interest in promoting interbrand competition. It is also interested in promoting the success of small business. Congress had declared the protection of small business to be the national policy and has charged this agency with the primary responsibility of implementing that policy. It is also our national policy to promote and protect free and open competition. These policies are not at odds with one another; they can readily be coordinated. It is only when they are regarded as absolutes to be invoked blindly and without regard to economic realities that conflict arises.

In urging the legality of the restrictions . . . we are not arguing for an antitrust exemption in favor of small business. Everyone agrees that if the protection of the small businessman were to require us to discard our entire philosophy of competition as the principal regulator of business affairs, the price would be much too high for society to pay. . . .

But it is possible to uphold these restrictions without denying society the fruits of competition in the slightest. No paradox inheres in this assertion. At no time in our Sherman law jurisprudence, nor indeed in the antecedent common law of the preceding two centuries has an agreement been deemed unlawful merely because it restrained competition. . . .

Unfortunately, there are some today who believe that any arrangement having any impact on competition, no matter how slight and no matter what the circumstances or reason, must be forbidden. Under their view, the fact that competition was restrained is the end of the inquiry. We, in the Brandeis tradition, believe that it is only the beginning.

It is our fundamental thesis that the restrictions we have considered strengthen our competitive institutions. They increase the vigor of interbrand competition. It must frankly be acknowledged that they eliminate intrabrand competition. What is needed is a sense of balance. Are the anticompetitive consequences resulting from the elimination of intrabrand competition outbalanced by the pro-competitive effects of a more vigorous and healthy interbrand competition? This in a nutshell is the issue. . . .

In studying the issues in terms of the relative social desirability of inter- as contrasted with intra-brand competition, we in our own thinking carefully eschew any indulgence in absolute and unqualified propositions. There may be instances where society requires more intrabrand competition than these restrictions permit. This is why we have a rule of reason, which takes all facts and circumstances into consideration. We would avoid either extreme of saying that these arrangements are always lawful or unlawful. Legality should depend upon the facts. . . .

PART V

Antitrust in Operation

A PARTIAL SEARCH FOR AFFIRMATIVE
ANTITRUST ANSWERS

William Simon

William Simon is an attorney-at-law practicing in Washington, D.C., and the author of numerous articles and addresses on antitrust problems.

. . . In my days in law school, evaluation of an important and novel legal problem required thorough research to predict how the Supreme Court would decide the question if and when presented to it. Today that is a relatively unimportant question in the search for antitrust answers. It is far more important to try to predict whether the Department of Justice or the Federal Trade Commission will attack the contemplated transaction. And it is critical to try to predict whether the Solicitor General will permit an appeal to the Supreme Court if suit is brought and a District Court decides against the Department, or a Court of Appeals decides against the Commission.

By statute no government agency may seek Supreme Court review of an adverse lower court decision without the approval of the Solicitor General. Since World War II, there have been many more antitrust cases in which the Solicitor General has refused to permit a government appeal to the Supreme Court than there have been cases in which the Supreme Court has held for a defendant.

In the slightly more than ten years between September, 1955, and

Fifth Annual Conference on Antitrust in an Expanding Economy (New York: National Industrial Conference Board, 1966), pp. 31-42. Copyright 1966, National Industrial Conference Board.

December, 1965, the Supreme Court decided 46 antitrust cases which had been brought by the Department of Justice. The Department was successful in 41 of the 46 cases. . . . It has now been more than seven years since the Supreme Court has decided a case against the Commission.

Since the passage of the 1950 antimerger law, there have been 10 merger cases before the Court, 9 brought by the Department and 1 by the Commission; and the government has won every one of them.

[From 1956 to 1966,] 19 private treble-damage cases have been before the Supreme Court; the Court decided 12 of those cases for the plaintiff and 7 for the defendant.

Public records do not reveal the precise number of cases in which the Solicitor General has refused the Commission or the Antitrust Division permission to appeal to the Supreme Court cases they lost. But these facts are known: (1) the Commission has lost many cases in the Courts of Appeals, and the Antitrust Division has lost many cases in the District Courts, which were not taken to the Supreme Court; (2) the Commission is always prone to seek Supreme Court review of an adverse decision and in many cases the trade press has reported that its efforts to do so have been rejected by the Solicitor General; (3) by and large, the Antitrust Division is no less eager to seek reversal of the cases it has lost; and (4) the Solicitor General has traditionally considered it his obligation to bring before the Supreme Court only those cases he considered of sufficient importance to warrant the time and attention of the Court.

The won and lost record in the lower courts of both the Commission and the Department is markedly different from their achievements in the Supreme Court. Relatively few of the cases brought by the Department actually go to trial, and it is not always possible clearly to define who won the case in the trial court. But in the cases the Department has tried in the District Courts [since 1956], it has lost about as many cases as it has won. Similarly, it is not always feasible to determine whether the Commission won or lost a case in the Court of Appeals. And a distinction must be made between Commission antitrust cases and those under Section 5 of the Trade Commission Act with an antitrust flavor, on the one hand, from its false and misleading advertising cases [on the other]. Numerically the latter have accounted for a large majority of the Commission's cases; and the Courts of Appeals have long been prone almost routinely to affirm the Commission in false advertising cases. But in the Commission's antitrust and related cases, it too has lost about as many cases in the Courts of Appeals as it has won.

The importance of the Solicitor General's role is illustrated by *American Oil Co. v. Federal Trade Commission.* The Court of Appeals for the Seventh Circuit had rejected the Commission's view that temporary price differences between competing gasoline dealers, in a significant amount, violated the Robinson-Patman Act. The Court held that the Act was violated only where the amount of the difference as well as its duration were sufficient to impair the ability of the disfavored customer to compete. The Commission considered this a substantial blow to its Robinson-Patman enforcement. In a petition to the Supreme Court for review of that decision, it said that it had a substantial number of cases, both in the formal and in the informal stage, which would be controlled by *American Oil.* Yet the Commission was required to state in its petition for review that, while the Solicitor General did not object to its seeking a Supreme Court review, he disagreed with the Commission on the merits and believed the case had been properly decided below. The Supreme Court promptly denied the Commission's petition for review.

The record appears, at least in part, to indicate that the Supreme Court has lost interest in cases involving government regulation of business—choosing largely to abdicate its judicial role to the "expertise" of government administrators. Presumably preoccupied with what it considers to be more important questions of the day, the Court appears to assume that government administrators carefully, and impartially, consider and correctly decide the legality of all business conduct. The Court appears oblivious to the fact that once their cases get to court, the government administrators are no less advocates than any other lawyer.

It is not possible to give meaningful statistics on the number of cases investigated by the Department or the Commission where a decision not to bring suit was made for economic, social or political reasons. But it is certain that such data, if available, as well as data on the number of cases which the Solicitor General refused to permit the Antitrust Division or the Commission to take to the Supreme Court, would demonstrate that it is far more important to business, in evaluating the propriety of proposed conduct, to attempt to predict the likelihood that the Department or the Commission will bring suit, and whether the Solicitor General will permit a Supreme Court review in the event of an adverse lower court decision, than it is to predict the Supreme Court's final decision.

Data released by the Commission discloses that there have [long] been more than a thousand mergers a year . . . over 1500 a year in recent years. Of course, the government could not have made out a case against many of those mergers no matter how hard it tried. But it is significant that in the 10-year period July 1, 1955, through June 30, 1965, the Department of Justice brought 96 cases alleging a violation of Section 7 of the Clayton Act—the anti-merger statute—and in that period the Commission brought 54 such cases, an average of 10 cases a year for the Department and 5 for the Commission. With less than 1½ per cent of the mergers made being attacked, the legal advisor's most difficult problem is to determine what mergers will, or will not, be attacked. . . .

In the search for Affirmative Antitrust Answers, we must first separate the hard-core violations such as price-fixing conspiracies, for which there is no legal justification under existing law, from those transactions which are commercially and economically justifiable and where legal guidelines are frequently obscure. In the latter category, which includes such areas as quantity pricing and expansion through acquisition, businessmen generally cannot export unequivocal answers from counsel. More important, they should not stop with asking whether the transaction is legal or illegal, but must weight the calculated risks in making the deal against those in not making the deal.

Mergers fall into three categories: (1) those undoubtedly legal, (2) those clearly illegal, and (3) a wide grey area in between in which no firm answer can be given. In those cases, it is necessary to forecast the risks involved if the acquisition should be attacked, and if the government should either win in the lower courts or lose below and be permitted a Supreme Court review by the Solicitor General.

If you are required to divest two to five years hence, what will the property bring compared to its cost? What profits or losses can you expect in operating the business during the period of litigation? What will be the cost and competitive problems after divestiture of establishing a comparable source of supply or distribution system, by internal expansion, if it is likely that it will then be necessary to do so? What other long-term advantages and disadvantages can be foreseen from the acquisition if divestiture is ultimately ordered? Where your competitors are integrating—either forward or backward—though acquisitions, what will be the likely cost to you of permitting them a two- to ten-year head start while you try to integrate through internal expansion? Finally, are there any alternative means of accomplishing the same objectives with lesser risks?

Into these calculations must also be factored the cost of litigation, both in terms of external expenses and internal manpower requirements, as well as the possible effects of an injunction against further acquisitions, for some period of time in some geographic and product area, which may be included in a decree of divestiture. Such an evaluation of the business risks in a merger may frequently be far more relevant and meaningful than an attempt to forecast the outcome of litigation over its legality.

While the Supreme Court's *Brown Shoe* decision was a great legal victory for the government, many are not aware of the fact that Brown sold the Kinney shoe properties to Woolworth for almost $20 million more than their cost. And, when the Department sued Phillips Petroleum to force it to divest itself of its holdings in Union Oil, Phillips sold that stock at a $25 million profit.

It is frequently possible to say with absolute certainty that certain conduct is unlawful, but in antitrust it is rarely possible to say with absolute certainty that any significant transaction is both lawful now and will be held lawful five or ten years hence.

Of course, businessmen can seek guidance in their antitrust problems from the Business Advisory Service of the Federal Trade Commission or under the Antitrust Business Review Procedures of the Department of Justice. But it is a rare case when it is desirable to seek a formal advisory opinion on proposed legal conduct from either the Commission or the Department.

The Commission has taken four to six months, and even longer, to give an answer. Frequently the commercial need for an answer then no longer exists. Moreover, Commission advisory opinions disclose little more than broad generalizations of unquestioned antitrust rules available to businessmen from any competent lawyer. The Commission has bent over backwards, in issuing advisory opinions, to establish no controversial precedents and to avoid committing itself on the propriety of questionable conduct. This is understandable. The Commission cannot know all the facts, or likely competitive effects, when issuing an advisory opinion. Yet, even though the validity of its opinions are expressly subject to the facts presented to it, the Commission subjects itself to Congressional and public criticism if approved conduct turns out to be unpopular —or if the known facts result in competitive injury. Clearance has been given in only the clearest cases.

Moreover, it is frequently undesirable for a businessman to expose to Commission scrutiny all of the facts relating to a transaction, frequently facts which might otherwise never have come to its attention and, in many cases, which the businessman subsequently wishes had not come to the Commission's attention.

There are cases, of course, when there is no alternative but to seek antitrust clearance. This may include the case in which a lender is unwilling to consummate a transaction without clearance or where for other valid reasons a deal cannot be closed without clearance. But the cases where this is either necessary or desirable represents a minimal fraction of the whole, and generally it is not prudent to seek an advisory opinion unless you are prepared to abide by the advice given.

These comments as to Commission advisory opinions have historically been equally true of the Department of Justice.

. . . Over the years both the Commission and the Department have consistently been unwilling to grant clearance for transactions on which they would never file suit if the transaction was consummated without a request for clearance. In those acquisitions which fall into the wide grey area discussed above, both the Commission and the Department have generally preferred not to commit themselves in advance but rather to wait until after the transaction is completed and they know whether there are any injured competitors who will be likely witnesses if the case goes to trial. . . .

If you find the search for Affirmative Antitrust Answers is not simple, it is because there are no simple affirmative answers to important transactions; the simple answers are generally either negative or on matters not of great significance. But the fact is that there is at least one company that has grown a hundred-fold through 50 acquisitions in the last ten years without a lawsuit. Uncertainty should not mean defeatism.

PART VI

Antitrust Abroad

COMPETITION IN THE COURT

N. H. Leyland

N. H. Leyland was formerly Lecturer in Economics at Brasenose College, Oxford University, and is now an economist with The Oxford Center of Economic Research.

It is not perhaps surprising that from the judgements of the Restrictive Practices Court it is not possible to distil a view of what that competition is with reference to which the practices of industries are to be judged. There is no model laid down in the Act. There is, instead, a presumption that agreements between manufacturers with respect to prices, terms, quantities, and processes of manufacture are against the public interest unless they can be shown to confer benefits. A more competitive state is defined implicitly as that state which would obtain if the restrictions were removed. But a more competitive state in this sense is not necessarily desirable. That is something the Court has to decide, and the decision has to be based in the last analysis upon a comparison between the circumstances that would obtain in the industry if the agreement went and those that do now obtain. The Court has to predict business behaviour.

But not only does it have to predict the economic consequences of that behaviour, it has to evaluate those consequences without any clear frame of reference. It cannot appeal to the Act. It cannot get a clear answer from economists, for discussion of the effects of

Oxford Economic Papers, XVII (1965), 461-467. Copyright 1965, Oxford University.

'imperfections' in the competitive process is ill-served by economic theory. Not only is much of the theory based on unrealistic assumptions, not only is the 'ideal' case itself bad theory, but we have no coherent, generally accepted theory about a firm's growth or the sources of innovation. We have, moreover, precious little empirical study.

In many ways therefore the Court's predictions are bound to be contained within a rather narrow area. If they were not, the evaluation problem would be impossibly difficult. Consider, for example, the following highly formalized sequence. An agreement keeps in being a fringe of small firms with smaller physical and financial resources than a group of large firms. The market structure may be characterized as oligopoly with imperfect competition. The small firms' existence, it is claimed, prevents the increasing monopolization of the industry and therefore keeps prices lower than they would be after successful monopolization. If the agreement goes, the large firms may drive out the small after a price war. To recoup the costs of that war they will raise prices and keep them permanently higher than they would have been if the agreement had remained in force. The number of predictions that has to be made in this case is clearly very large. Yet this is essentially a simple case.

But the most relevant predictions of all for public policy are, what will the cost structure of the industry be after re-organization and to what extent will the margin between cost and price in the new situation be susceptible to potential competition? If the determination of an agreement lowers the costs of the industry, whether it be by the exploitation of economies of scale, reduction of selling costs, or rationalization of the product range, or simply because the lowest cost firms expand output, then there will be benefit even though there may have been in some technical sense an increase in the degree of monopoly. But how can these predictions be made? The uncertainties surrounding them are very great. It has emerged very clearly from the cases in the Court that many firms have a very poor idea indeed of their costs and how costs behave when output changes, even when allowance is made for the difficulties of costing products in a multi-product firm. When the existing costs cannot be agreed, discussion of the costs that would prevail if the industry structure were changed must appear and indeed be purely academic.

What is required is a set of tests for adequate business performance. While I do not suggest that these should be embodied in an amendment to the Act, I feel that such a set has not emerged from the activities of the Court.

What criteria should be used? What are the important questions to ask? It should be possible to answer the following with reference to the history of the industry and its present circumstances and to establish by weighting the answers a presumption about the public aspects of the industry's performance. No single test on its own is likely to be of use. The application of them all will not be universally appropriate.

1. Profits

The profits test is an important one. The Monopolies Commission has used as a measure of profitability the rate of gross profit on capital employed. While there are many difficulties in measuring the capital employed and many equally sensible definitions are possible, it should be possible to agree on a definition for use in each particular case. If the definition makes comparison with the published figures impossible, then two sets of figures can be used, of which one would be consistent with the definition used in Economic Trends. The industry's rate should be compared also with that of industries with similar growth rates if such there be. One would not expect an industry experiencing a secular decline in demand to have the same average rate as one with a rising output trend. In real life the adjustment to what are essentially disequilibrium situations may take a very long time. It is therefore important to study the trend of profit rates and their dispersion.

2. Cost/price relationships

How rapidly are cost changes reflected in price changes? Do prices fluctuate more than cost elements and if so, why? On the whole the Court has come down in favour of agreements which tie the price to some cost formula and against those where the linkage is weak, or the costs inadequately assessed. But we need to know rather more than whether the price-fixing formula is based on an adequate set of costings. We should know also whether the same firms are consistently the lowest-cost firms and if so whether they extend their share of the market. If they do not, is it because costs would rise with output, or is it because the competitive arrangements prevent them from doing so?

3. Cost structure

What are the major cost elements and how have they changed? One of the effects of agreements may be expected to be a change in cost structure. If competition by price is ruled out, then selling and advertising costs may increase. It is important therefore to discover changes in the cost structure over time and to assess the extent to which these are the results of any price agreement. Comparisons can be made either with the same industry in other countries or with industries serving similar markets which have no agreement. [The Court does not like comparisons with other industries or countries.]

4. Capacity/output relationships

Is investment excessive or deficient in relation to output? It is of course important in this context to relate the imbalance to a time scale. How often and over what period do imbalances occur? What happens when investment is consistently deficient, do imports rise, order books lengthen, or prices rise? How responsive are the investment decisions of firms to the imbalance? How rapidly does disinvestment occur when capacity is excessive?

5. Buyer/seller relationships

What are the relative bargaining strengths of buyers and sellers? Have there been significant shifts in these? How have the shifts affected negotiations? This seems to me to be a relatively neglected aspect of the competitive process and the proceedings in the Court have not thrown much light on it. A very large number of transactions are conducted between firms or between the government or its agencies and firms.

6. Entry

Is entry into the market easy? What are the barriers to entry? Does the identity of the firms change? Where a market is served mainly by multi-product firms, do the shares going to the various firms change?

7. *Progressiveness*

What is the industry's record in product and process innovation? Do competitive arrangements hinder change? What is the expenditure on research? There are unfortunately no simple indicators of product progressiveness. There are, however, some indicators of process innovation. It may be useful to examine physical indicators such as the growth of productivity per man hour, changes in fuel and material input per unit of output, and of investment per head.

It is in the nature of these last two tests that the questions they entail should be both the most important to ask and the most difficult to answer.

It may be that if one were to aggregate the cases that have so far been before the Court all these tests have with various degrees of thoroughness been applied. I believe, however, that they should be systematically applied in every case, because they make explicit the aspects of business behaviour which have to be balanced before one can arrive at a satisfactory answer as to whether or not an industry's performance is as good as it can be. There is an argument (sometimes couched in almost mystical terms) which appears with great frequency in the cases, namely that the agreement encourages inter-firm confidence with consequential advantages which may take the form of co-operation in research, the preservation of quality, standardization, or the encouragement of investment. It is this type of argument which it is most important to submit to as many tests and comparisons as possible.

CONCLUSION

The early judgements were fierce. Some observers believe that there has been a gradual softening. Early severity was probably essential, as the 1956 Act marked a new approach to the competitive system. Had all the early cases passed successfully through the Court, it is highly likely that most of the cases on the Register would have been fought. The climate of opinion both in Parliament and in industry was, on the whole, favourable to change.

None the less after eight years of operation it is clear that certain disadvantages of the Court and its procedures need examination and, if possible, alteration. The shock therapy has been administered. Industry has been forced to examine its practices and more than half the agreements have been abandoned without testing in the Court. The following disadvantages come from the fact that cases are brought before a superior Court.

(*a*) Proceedings are adversary. This means above all that witnesses cannot agree together beforehand the ground that is common to them, emphasizing only the points of difference and the reasons for those differences. This is particularly important in the case of the evidence of economists and accountants. Cross-examination is not the best method of bringing out the implications of economic rationalization. Either expert witnesses should be instructed to prepare a common document, together with a summary of their disagreements and a statement of the reasons for them, or the Court should have the services of an economist, either as a lay judge or as an assistant to the judges.

(*b*) Evidence may be, and often is, brought in at the last minute during the hearing. If the industry really believes that its case can be argued it should have the arguments and information available in good time, so that the Registrar and his witnesses have a chance of considering them.

(*c*) The Court judges an agreement as it is. It cannot recommend how an agreement should be altered so as to remove its harmful elements. . . . Any constructiveness can only arise from the establishment of case law which would enable industry to frame its agreements in such a way and to such an end as would ensure their surviving inspection by the Court. But it would be very hard indeed to argue that from the cases so far it is possible to describe the kind of agreement which would survive.

(*d*) The Court cannot police agreements. In a way the Registrar is, among all his other duties, the Court's policeman. But he has to consider mainly the extent to which the industry is obeying the Court's judgement. If the industry desires a new agreement embodying only the elements which the Court had not condemned, a new registration and a new hearing would presumably be necessary. Cases are expensive not only in terms of the cost of fees but more importantly in the opportunity cost of senior executives' time.

(*e*) There is no provision under existing arrangements for pro-posed schemes to be cleared. Suppose, for example, it was decided to set up an agreement to rationalize production in an industry where economies of scale were important, so that firm A or firms A and B would produce only size X, firm C or firms C, D, and E, size Z, and so on, how could the industry know whether this agreement would pass through the Court and when? The agreement would have to be established first and put into operation before it could be judged. It would not be impossible to give agreements a trial period after which they would be inspected with respect to certain pre-stated criteria selected from the tests outlined above. A Court, however, clearly cannot do this.

(*f*) Perhaps most important of all is the consideration that there is no adequate follow-up. If an agreement passes through the Court, any variation of that agreement or any change in the circum-stances justifies a new reference. Yet some changes may be very desirable. Many agreements that have passed could, with great benefit to the achievement of their stated ends, as well as to the public interest, be greatly improved. Moreover, if some set of tests such as I have proposed were to be adopted it would be necessary to have a rather large department engaged upon empirical study of industries without agreement, industries where agreements have been abandoned, and similar industries in other countries. I believe that some such body is essential. At the moment the industry selects the ground upon which it will fight for its agreement, the Registrar selects the ground upon which he will try to establish detriment. But it should be a matter of form that certain kinds of evidence (e.g. about profitability, productivity, cost-structure, and changes in the share of the market of different firms) are presented whether the industry proposes to rely upon this evidence or not.

In short, the Court has performed well within the limitations of an Act which did not lay down any performance tests. Now it is necessary to modify the rigidity of operation that may have arisen from the procedures and precedents of a Court.

LIST OF CASES MENTIONED IN TEXT

A. G. Spalding & Bros., Inc. v. *FTC*, 301 F. 2d 585 (3rd Cir., 1962).

American Crystal Sugar Co. v. *The Cuban-American Sugar Co.*, 152 F. Supp. 387 (S.D.N.Y., 1957), aff'd 259 F. 2d 524 (2nd Cir., 1958).

American Oil Co. v. *FTC*, 325 F. 2d 101 (7th Cir., 1963).

American Tobacco Co. v. *U.S.*, 328 U.S. 781 (1946).

Apex Hosiery Co. v. *Leader*, 310 U.S. 469 (1940).

Appalachian Coals, Inc. v. *U.S.*, 288 U.S. 344 (1933).

Beit v. *Beit*, 63 A. 2d 161 (1948).

Brown Shoe Co. v. *U.S.*, 370 U.S. 294 (1962).

Bruce's Juices, Inc. v. *American Can Co.*, 330 U.S. 743 (1947).

Chicago Board of Trade v. *U.S.*, 246 U.S. 23 (1918).

Crown Zellerbach Corp. v. *FTC*, 296 F. 2d 800 (9th Cir., 1961).

Eastman Kodak Co. v. *Southern Photo Materials Co.*, 273 I?S? 359 (1927).

Ethyl Gasoline v. *U.S.*, 309 U.S. 436 (1940).

FTC v. *Cement Inst.*, 333 U.S. 683 (1948).

FTC v. *Consolidated Foods*, 380 U.S. 592 (1965).

FTC v. *Dean Foods Co.*, 348 U.S. 597 (1966).

FTC v. *R. F. Keppel & Bros., Inc.*, 291 U.S. 304 (1934).

Foremost Dairies, Inc., 60 F.T.C. 914 (1963).

Hamilton Watch Co. v. *Benrus Watch Co.*, 114 F. Supp. 307 (D. Conn., 1953), aff'd 206 F. 2d 738 (2d Cir., 1953).

Hartford Empire Co. v. *U.S.*, 323 U.S. 386 (1945).

Holophane Co. v. *U.S.*, 352 U.S. 903 (1956).

International Salt Co. v. *U.S.*, 280 U.S. 291 (1930).

Kelly v. *Kosuga*, 358 U.S. 516 (1959).

Northern Pac. Ry. v. *U.S.*, 356 U.S. 1 (1958).

Northern Sec. Co. v. *U.S.*, 193 U.S. 197 (1904).

Packard Motor Car Co. v. *Webster Motor Car Co.*, 243 F. 2d 418 (D.C. Cir., 1957).

Pan American World Airways, Inc. v. *U.S.*, 371 U.S. 296 (1963)

Procter & Gamble Co. v. *FTC*, 358 F. 2d 74 (6th Cir., 1966).

Radovich v. *Nat. Football League*, 352 U.S. 445 (1957).

Scott Paper Co. v. *FTC*, 301 F. 2d 579 (3rd Cir., 1962).

Standard Fashion Co. v. *Magrane-Houston Co.*, 258 U.S. 346 (1922).

Standard Oil Co. v. *U.S.*, 221 U.S. 1 (1911).

Standard Oil Co. (Cal.) v. *U.S.*, 337 U.S. 293 (1949).

Standard Oil Co. (Ind.) v. *U.S.*, 283 U.S. 163 (1931).

Standard Sanitary Mfg. Co. v. *U.S.*, 226 U.S. 20 (1912).

Summerhays v. *Scher*, 52 P. 2d 512 (1935).

Tampa Elec. Co. v. *Nashville Coal Co.*, 365 U.S. 320 (1961).

U.S. v. *Aluminum Co. of America*, 148 F. 2d 416 (2d Cir., 1945).

U.S. v. *Aluminum Co. of America*, 377 U.S. 277 (1964).

U.S. v. *American Tobacco Co.*, 221 U.S. 106 (1911).

U.S. v. *Bethlehem Steel Corp.*, 168 F. Supp. 576 (S.D.N.Y., 1958).

U.S. v. *Blass & Laughlin, Inc.*, 202 F. Supp. 334 (S.D. Calif., 1962).

U.S. v. *Columbia Steel Co.*, 334 U.S. 495 (1948).

U.S. v. *Continental Can Co.*, 378 U.S. 441 (1964).

U.S. v. *Corn Products Ref. Co.*, 234 Fed. 964 (S.D.N.Y., 1916).

U.S. v. *E.I. du Pont de Nemours & Co.*, 366 U.S. 316 (1961).

U.S. v. *E.I. du Pont de Nemours & Co.*, 188 Fed. 127 (D.C. Del., 1911).

U.S. v. *El Paso Natural Gas Co.*, 376 U.S. 651 (1964).

U.S. v. *First Nat. Bank of Lexington*, 376 U.S. 665 (1964).

U.S. v. *General Elec. Co.*, 272 U.S. 476 (1926).

U.S. v. *General Elec. Co.*, 80 F. Supp. 989 (S.D.N.Y., 1948).

U.S. v. *Kennecott Copper Corp.*, 231 F. Supp. 95 (S.D.N.Y., 1964).

U.S. v. *Lever Bros. Co.*, 216 F. Supp. 887 (S.D.N.Y., 1963).

U.S. v. *Loew's, Inc.*, 371 U.S. 38 (1962).

U.S. v. *Nat. Lead Co.*, 332 U.S. 319 (1947).

U.S. v. *Newmont Mining Corp.*, 34 F.R.D. 117 (S.D.N.Y., 1964).

U.S. v. *Pabst Brewing Co.*, 384 U.S. 546 (1966).

U.S. v. *Paramount Pictures, Inc.*, 334 U.S. 141 (1948).

U.S. v. *Penn-Olin Chem. Co.*, 378 U.S. 158 (1964).

U.S. v. *Philadelphia Nat. Bank*, 374 U.S. 321 (1963).

U.S. v. *Safeway Stores, Inc.*, 20 F.R.D. 451 (N.D. Tex., 1957).

U.S. v. *Sears, Roebuck & Co.*, 111 F. Supp. 614 (S.D.N.Y., 1953).

SUGGESTED READINGS

Adams, Walter, ed., *The Structure of American Industry*, 3rd ed. (New York: The Macmillan Company, 1961).

Adelman, Morris A., "An Economist Looks at the Sherman Act," *A.B.A. Antitrust Section* (1965), p. 40.

————, *A&P: Study in Cost Price Behavior and Public Policy* (Cambridge, Mass.: Harvard University Press, 1959).

Attorney-General's Committee, Report of the (Washington: Government Printing Office, 1955).

Bain, Joe S., *Barriers to New Competition* (Cambridge, Mass.: Harvard University Press, 1956).

————, *Industrial Organization* (New York: John Wiley & Sons, 1959).

————, "Price Leaders, Barometers and Kinks," *The Journal of Business*, XXXIII (1960), 195ff.

Barnes, Irston R., "The Role of the Economist in Merger Cases," *Antitrust Bulletin*, III (1958), 505ff.

Baumol, William J., *Business Behavior, Value and Growth*, 2nd ed. (New York: Harcourt, Brace & World, 1967).

Berle, Adolf A., *The Twentieth Century Capitalist Revolution* (New York: Harcourt, Brace & World, 1954).

Bork, Robert H., "The Rule of Reason and the Per Se Concept; Price-Fixing and Market Division," *Yale Law Journal*, LXXIV (1965), 775ff.

Boulding, Kenneth E., and George J. Stigler, eds., *Readings in Price Theory* (Homewood, Ill.: Richard D. Irwin, Inc., 1952).

Brewster, Kingman, Jr., *Antitrust and American Business Abroad* (New York: McGraw-Hill Book Company, 1958).

Cardozo, Benjamin Nathan, *The Nature of the Judicial Process* (New Haven, Conn.: Yale University Press, 1921).

Caves, Richard E., *American Industry: Structure, Conduct, Performance*, 2nd ed. (Englewood Cliffs, N.J.: Prentice-Hall, Inc., 1967).

Chadwell, John T., "Competition and Section 1 of the Sherman Act," *A.B.A. Antitrust Section,* XXVII (1965), 68ff.

Chamberlin, Edward H., ed., *Monopoly and Competition and Their Regulation* (London: St. Martin's Press, 1954).

——, *The Theory of Monopolistic Competition,* 8th ed. (Cambridge, Mass.: Harvard University Press, 1962).

Clark, John Maurice, *Competition as a Dynamic Process* (Washington: The Brookings Institution, 1961).

——, "Toward a Theory of Workable Competition," *American Economic Review,* XXX (1940), 241ff.

Edwards, Corwin D., *The Price Discrimination Law* (Washington: The Brookings Institution, 1959).

Fellner, William J., *Competition Among the Few* (New York: Augustus M. Kelley, 1949).

Galbraith, John Kenneth, *American Capitalism: The Concept of Countervailing Power* (Boston: Houghton Mifflin Co., 1952).

Grether, E.T., "Economic Analysis and Antitrust Enforcement," *Antitrust Bulletin,* IV (1959), 55ff.

Handler, Milton, "Nineteenth Annual Review of Recent Antitrust Developments," *Record,* XXI (1966), 539ff.

Hanson, J.J., "Comparison of State and Federal Antitrust Laws in Selected Areas," *A.B.A. Antitrust Section,* XXIX (1965), 267ff.

Hefflebower, Richard B., and George W. Stocking, eds., *Readings in Industrial Organization and Public Policy* (Homewood, Ill.: Richard D. Irwin, Inc., 1958).

Jaffe, Louis L., "Primary Jurisdiction," *Harvard Law Review,* LXXVII (1964), 1037ff.

Kaysen, Carl, *United States* v. *United Shoe Machinery Corporation* (Cambridge, Mass.: Harvard University Press, 1956).

——, and Donald J. Turner, *Antitrust Policy: An Economic and Legal Analysis* (Cambridge, Mass.: Harvard University Press, 1959).

——, and Jesse W. Markham, "The Present War on Bigness I, II," Fourth Conference on Antitrust in an Expanding Economy (New York: National Industrial Conference Board, 1965), p. 38ff.

Keyes, Lucile Sheppard, "Price Discrimination in Law and Economics," *Southern Economic Journal,* XXVII (1961), 320ff.

Kuenne, Robert E., ed., *Monopolistic Competition Theory: Studies in Impact* (New York: John Wiley & Sons, 1967).

Lerner, Abba P., "The Concept of Monopoly and the Measurement of Monopoly Power," *Review of Economic Studies,* I (1934), 157ff.

Levi, Edward, "The Monopoly Problem as Viewed by a Lawyer," *American Economic Review Supplement,* XLII (1957), 293ff.

Low, Richard E., *American Economic Organization* (Homewood, Ill.: Richard D. Irwin, 1968).

———, "The Failing Company Doctrine: An Illusive Economic Defense Under Section 7 of the Clayton Act," *Fordham Law Review,* XXXV (1967), 425ff.

Mason, Edward S., *Economic Concentration and the Monopoly Problem* (Cambridge, Mass.: Harvard University Press, 1957).

———, *The Corporation in Modern Society* (Cambridge, Mass.: Harvard University Press, 1960).

Massel, Mark S., *Competition and Monopoly: Legal and Economic Issues* (Garden City, N.Y.: Doubleday & Co., 1964).

National Bureau of Economic Research, ed., *Business Concentration and Price Policy* (Princeton, N.J.: Princeton University Press, 1955).

Neale, A.D., *The Antitrust Laws of the United States of America* (New York: Cambridge University Press, 1960).

Osborne, Dale K., "The Role of Entry in Oligopoly Theory," *The Journal of Political Economy,* LXXII (1964) 396ff.

Robinson, Joan, *The Economics of Imperfect Competition* (New York: St. Martin's Press, 1934).

Schumpeter, Joseph A., *Capitalism, Socialism and Democracy,* 3rd ed. (New York: Harper & Row, Publishers, 1950).

Spier, Leo, "Restrictive Business Practices and Competition in the European Economic Community," *California Law Review,* LIII (1965), 1337ff.

Stigler, George J., *The Theory of Price,* 3rd ed. (New York: The Macmillan Company, 1966).

Stocking, George W., "Economic Change and the Sherman Act: Some Reflections on 'Workable Competition,'" *Virginia Law Review,* XII (1958), 537ff.

———, *Workable Competition and Antitrust Policy* (Nashville, Tenn.: Vanderbilt University Press, 1961).

Sunderland, Arthur, "Economics in the Restrictive Practices Court," *Oxford Economic Papers,* XVII (1965), 385ff.

Van Cise, Jerrold G., *The Federal Antitrust Laws,* 2nd ed. (Washington: American Enterprise Association, 1965).

Webster, Bethuel M., "The Use of Economic Experts in Antitrust Litigation," *Record*, XVII (1962), 456ff.

Whitney, Simon N., *Antitrust Policies* (New York: Twentieth Century Fund, 1958).